"I'm a big believer that sports teach us many of the most spiritual lessons we can learn in life. Cory Reese has written a deeply personal memoir about overcoming depression with the healing lessons he learned as an ultramarathon runner. Whether you are a runner or not, the profound lessons in this book translate to all areas of life. *Stronger Than the Dark* is a powerful story of overcoming adversity with grit, courage, and unflinching honesty."

~ Darrin Donnelly, bestselling author of *Think Like a Warrior*

"In his new book *Stronger Than the Dark*, Cory Reese opens up about depression in a way that readers can immediately relate to. Reese shows us that even a hardened ultra marathoner can struggle in life. He demonstrates that there is strength in vulnerability. Anyone who has struggled with depression will be comforted by the constant message that we have nothing to be ashamed of, and that we are not alone."

~ Kara Goucher, two-time Olympian, and author of *Strong*

"Riveting and propulsive, Cory Reese proves that you needn't fear the darkness if you have the light inside."

~ Dean Karnazes, ultramarathoner and NY Times bestselling author

"*Stronger Than the Dark* is a jaw-dropping glimpse into the personal struggles of one of our favorite and most upbeat ultrarunning personalities. Cory's journey to find his path out of the darkness is an inspiration to anyone who struggles, in running, or in life."

~ Scott Kummer, Ten Junk Miles Podcast

"Cory Reese's *Stronger Than the Dark* is worth its weight in gold--honest, funny, heartfelt, and ultimately inspiring."

~ Matt Fitzgerald, author of *Life Is a Marathon*

"*Stronger Than the Dark* is an amazing story. Cory touches on a subject so many live in silence with: depression. His journey teaches that it's okay to not be okay, and you can get through those dark times."

~ Catra Corbett, author of *Reborn on the Run*

"Cory Reese, arguably the most endearing and funny character in the ultrarunning community, has written a powerful sequel to his earlier books that reveals the complexity of his personal struggles and confronts the reality that running long distances won't solve all his problems. While still delivering one-liners that will make readers laugh out loud, *Stronger than the Dark* unpacks the serious, sneaky and debilitating symptoms of depression, and details how a 314-mile footrace became the beginning of a journey to get help. Facing a personal crisis of faith and an unexpected rare illness, Cory keeps running ultras not to escape or suppress his feelings, but rather to enhance his ability to cope and to open up about them."

~ Sarah Lavender Smith, ultrarunning coach and author of
*The Trail Runner's Companion: A Step-by-Step Guide to
Trail Running and Racing, from 5Ks to Ultras*

"Cory's ability to weave heartwarming stories of running, family and friendship throughout his battle with depression are captivating. He exposes readers to an emotional rawness while tackling some of the hardest moments of his life, and yet continues to find courage and the ability to laugh during the toughest of times. This book is a must read for everyone."

~ Amy A. Clark, editor of *UltraRunning* Magazine

"*Stronger Than The Dark* is a beautiful, powerful examination of what happens when we realize that there doesn't need to be a bright light at the end of the tunnel for the tunnel to be awesome. Running, and other hard things make us vulnerable, and in that vulnerability is our true strength. Cory's strength made us explore our own, giving a beautiful reminder: we are in this together, and we've got this."

~ David Roche, author of *The Happy Runner*

"Many times, one does not know how much is within until mayhem strikes. When one can overcome adversity in sport and life, the satisfaction is even greater. In *Stronger than the Dark*, Cory brilliantly and beautifully illustrates how to love your comeback – and yourself in the process."

~ Jim Afremow, author of *The Champion's Mind*

STRONGER
— *Than the* —
DARK

An exploration of the intimate relationship between
running and depression

Cory Reese

Layout by Rachel Greene for elfinpen designs
Cover design by Syril Lagapa Pulido
Author photo by Rex Jones

Paperback ISBN: 978-1-7369664-0-2
eBook ISBN: 978-1-7369664-1-9

Some names and details have been changed to maintain patient confidentiality.

INTRODUCTION

I may be a Wheaties box reject, but I won't go down without a fight. The fat lady might as well just pack up her shit and go home, because there's no way I'm letting her sing. I have running to thank for helping me develop some fierce tenacity.

I've noticed that the simple act of running has a way of peeling open your soul. It doesn't matter whether you're on the road, on a trail, on a training run, or in the middle of a race. It's as if the fresh air creates an intimate vulnerability where runners talk about things you wouldn't normally talk about in the real world. Ask anyone who has been out on a group run, and they will verify the accuracy of this.

More than just an activity to burn some calories, running with a friend is essentially a sweaty, smelly therapy session. For a while, let's imagine we're out on a run together. Let's talk about the hard things, the things people are trying to heal from, the things that are difficult to discuss.

The book you are holding in your hand at this very moment is not the story I intended to write. Initially, I planned to write exclusively about my experience running the Vol State 500k, a 314 mile ultramarathon across Tennessee.

I wanted to use that adventure to highlight tools that can give you the mental toughness of an undaunted warrior. I planned to explore strategies for overcoming adversity, strengthening resilience, and how to endure when things get hard.

But that story took an unexpected turn after two life-changing things happened. First, I began to experience distressing health problems, and was eventually diagnosed with a chronic illness. Second, I had a traumatic parting with the Mormon church in which I had been raised for my entire life. I'll tell you about these events because they set a crisis in motion.

Science and psychology have long recognized the connection between depression and chronic health conditions. The link between depression and religious disaffiliation is a newer, but consequential, phenomenon. A chronic illness and a faith crisis were like two trains speeding toward each other, while I stood in the middle of the track. They initiated a freefall into what would become a crippling battle against depression.

The thing is, I was masterfully skilled at hiding that depression. My coworkers, friends, and even my family didn't know about the darkness that was following me. There's a phrase to describe that storm raging below the glossy surface: smiling depression. The outside looks happy and content, while the inside looks like a category 5 hurricane that is swirling around collecting all the rusty sheds in the neighborhood. I could have presented an authoritative TED Talk called "How to push down all your insecurities and painful feelings like a pro." Things aren't always what they seem.

I would have preferred to have this book be only about running, but a story like that would have been incomplete. Running is deeply intertwined with so many other things. Granted, that race across Tennessee was a pivotal experience that started me down a path of healing. But beyond running, this book explores the raw vulnerability of admitting that you're broken, and gathering the courage to ask for help. It's about learning how to fight back, and how to find the strength to keep putting one foot in front of the other when the voices in your head are yelling that you should quit.

Maybe it's just the testosterone talking, but I never really liked the word "vulnerable." "Vulnerable" is a tortoise that has been flipped on his back, unable to roll over, and is just waiting to become a coyote's bedtime snack. Why would anyone willingly want to do that? My approach has always been "Vulnerability? Um … no thanks. I'll pass." And yet, somehow, I allowed myself to go to that place of openness while writing.

When the depression hanging over me was at its darkest, it never occurred to me that many of the tools for mental toughness that I've learned through running could also be used to battle against the negativity and despair I was feeling. That didn't become clear until the sun began to rise and the darkness began to fade.

Why is depression so damn uncomfortable to talk about? Why is the topic so awkward and embarrassing? It's not like you're in middle school and your mom opens the door of the dressing room at JC Penny thinking you've already put on some potential new school clothes, but really, you're just standing there in your tighty whiteys. (Yep. That happened to me.) It's not like you're taking someone's blood pressure at the doctor's office and your runny nose accidentally drips onto your patient's arm. (Yep. That happened to my wife.) Depression shouldn't be embarrassing to talk about, right? But for me, and a lot of other professionals in the art of pushing down uncomfortable feelings, it is. It just is.

Some people feel the ebbs and flows of depression for longer than they can remember. That's not me. I've always been a happy person, full of hope and optimism. The despair I experienced came up quickly, triggered by those two life-changing experiences: developing a chronic illness, and leaving my church. I'll go into depth on both of those circumstances to show just how shattering they were. Those events initiated a darkness that took me by surprise.

Depression snuck up behind me when I wasn't expecting it. It's like I was walking down a dark alley one night, minding my own business, when depression popped out from behind a car and started bashing my kneecaps with nun chucks. I yelled "Hey! Come on, knock it off!" Then depression pulled out some brass knuckles and started punching me below the belt. So not cool. It wasn't until he started hurling a handful of razor-sharp throwing stars that I realized depression is an actual ninja. He is a stealthy, abusive ninja who has the ability to sneak up on you and attack. And depression doesn't fight fair. I was unarmed and unprepared for combat.

In the midst of my dark alley brawl with depression, there were a bunch of questions I wondered about:

- Why is it so hard to feel good enough?
- Why is it so hard to be honest about how we really feel?
- Why do we try so hard to act strong and hide insecurities?
- When the darkness of depression is trying to suffocate you, how do you find the light?

Within these pages, I will attempt to tackle these questions. My unique perspective comes from having sat on both sides of the therapy couch. I have been the one seeking help, as well as the one providing help as a therapist. That has given me insight into just how deceptive and overpowering depression can be.

If you've already managed to find your way out of the darkness and into the light, I'm proud of you. I know just how much strength it takes to pull yourself out of a dark place. If you're still stuck in the shadows, I hope you'll find some weapons here that will help you fight your battle until sunrise.

Bear with me on the emotional highs and lows within these pages. Over the course of writing the book, there were plenty of happy and funny experiences. There were also some times that were downright heavy. My friend, Luke, described these ups and downs perfectly: "It's like eating a fancy steak dinner and then being served a bag of cotton candy for dessert." These ups and downs are the essence of dealing with depression. You can be on top of the world, and then suddenly feel like you're in freefall inside an elevator whose rope just snapped. It can happen so quickly.

The highs are really high, and the lows are really low. As uncomfortable as it is, I didn't want to sugarcoat anything. So, within these pages, you'll see the view from both the peaks and the valleys.

I want to confront depression's favorite lie: that you are alone. Here is the reason I decided to write this book: opening up and removing the secrecy of depression saved me. Vulnerability liberated me. It's the act of giving voice to depression that begins to clear the fog. If you've been suffering in silence like I have, I hope this story strengthens your courage to open up. Depression has a sneaky way of making you feel isolated and alone. You trick yourself into believing that you're the only one who feels this way. But when you muster the courage to speak up and ask for help, you realize that you aren't so alone after all.

Fortunately, as runners, we have one ace up our sleeve. We have a unique advantage against life's pain and heartbreak: we know how to suffer.

ONE

I never imagined my life could feel so broken.

On the outside, a deceptive smile misleads people into thinking I'm happy. But on the inside, I feel like a smoldering dumpster fire. Is this what depression feels like? Am I just going through a midlife crisis? Because if this is, in fact, a midlife crisis, I've picked quite the doozie.

Some people quit their job. Some file for divorce, or buy an expensive sports car, or get a tattoo. I am facing my existential crisis by sitting in a cafe next to a guy who has Maxi Pads taped to his thighs.

My legs have been in perpetual forward motion for twenty-four hours as I watch the sun rise over Huntingdon, Tennessee. The sun's beaming rays are so stifling and thick that I could braid them into a golden ponytail. As I open the door to AJ's All Star Cafe, I can hear my stomach snarling like an irritable Chihuahua.

I receive a hearty welcome from the bubbly waitress in the lobby. She has more energy in her pinky finger than I have in my entire body. The lobby divides two separate dining rooms. On the left side of the restaurant, a ceiling fan is spinning above laminated tables that are supposed to look like wood. Men with wrinkly skin, slightly-too-tight plaid shirts, and cowboy hats, sit laughing and drinking cups of coffee. They must be the locals.

The right side of the restaurant is lonely and dim. It's impossible to know how long those burned-out lightbulbs have been waiting to be replaced. The only two occupants on the sad side of the restaurant are quiet and somber, like they are doing their best to hold back tears at a funeral. My feelings aren't hurt when the waitress ushers me to the right side of the restaurant. I know that if anyone on the happy side catches a whiff of my incinerated, putrid body, they will promptly lose their appetite.

I sit down next to a woman and man, their hydration packs resting on the table like rotting sacks of garbage. They clearly know each other well because they aren't engaging in introductory small talk. I introduce myself and ask "Are you guys married?" The woman says "Well, we will be soon. He just proposed to me." They look like they are each suffering from a raging case of narcolepsy, too exhausted to feel excited.

I shake my head trying to wiggle loose the cobwebs of sleep deprivation. I couldn't have heard her right. "Wait. Like ... you just proposed to her ... here in AJ's All Star Cafe?" He tells me that he began the race with a wedding ring hidden in the bottom of his hydration pack. They are doing the race together, and he felt like the second day of the race, stinky from twenty-four hours of heat in the same clothes, with salt crusted under his eyes, was the perfect time to ask a woman to spend the rest of her life with him. Only five minutes earlier, she agreed. I have no idea whether this is super romantic or the warning sign of an impending divorce.

"How are you guys feeling?" I ask. Immediately, I wish I could go back in time and un-ask such a foolish question. We have been running for 66 miles. Asking them how they are feeling after a 66-mile death slog is like asking "How are you feeling?" to someone who just got kicked in the groin by a llama. And that's when I see a horror that will forever be etched into my brain.

As soon as I ask the question, the guy pulls up the bottom of his shorts. His legs are so badly chaffed that he has Maxi Pads taped to the inside of his thighs. And there is still blood soaking through the pads. I think, "Thank you, your honor. No further questions." Sirens go off in my mind, and I hear my brain shout "WHAT. IN. THE. ACTUAL. FUUUUUUDGE." (Except that my brain doesn't say "fudge.") This … THIS … is the precise moment when I realize just how broken I must be, if I am willing to run a 314-mile race in hopes of putting the pieces of my life back together and finding peace.

I know the healing power of running. I know that when your only objective is forward motion, and you don't have all the other distractions of everyday life, twisted thoughts can get untangled. I know that when you face a potentially insurmountable challenge, you learn things about yourself that you couldn't learn otherwise. And I know the fulfillment that comes when things get hard but you don't give up, you don't back down.

Leading up to the race, I've been feeling like the foundation of my life is crumbling underneath me. I've been feeling lost and alone. I suppose that when I signed up to run an ultramarathon across Tennessee, I was hoping I'd find myself again somewhere along the steps of that odyssey. Nobody told me when I signed up that I would be sitting here in a cafe next to a guy who has Maxi Pads taped to his thighs.

Two

Once upon a time, my life was exceptionally ordinary. Well, as ordinary as possible when you have three teenagers living in your house, and every day feels like we're running the Big Top Circus. Our youngest daughter, Kylee, is the acrobat. She is always jumping, spinning, requesting the fanciest, hippest clothes, and providing the arena with constant energy and excitement as she comes up with creative ways to ask if she can borrow the car keys.

One year older, Dani is the circus clown. She knows how to make people smile and laugh, and has a radiating sense of happiness. She is always darting from one place to the next, whether it's school, work, a date, or water polo practice.

Jackson is two years older, and acts as the resident tight rope walker. Not only is he balancing his many obligations as a high school senior, but he also has to balance the tenuous moods of his teenage sisters, who have the capability of instantly turning into lions.

I am the amateur plate spinner. I'm trying to keep my work, family, running, and writing plates spinning without letting any of them fall. Sometimes, I try to get one wobbly plate back on track and end up dropping all of them.

And Mel is our heroic ring leader. She's always aware of everyone's schedules, is an amazing cook, an amazing wife and mom, a compassionate friend, and an amazing whistler of Macklemore songs, all while maintaining her busy job as a nurse practitioner.

Aside from the usual craziness of life, the biggest challenge we faced was the simple fact that all three kids were teenagers, and all three teenagers were living under the same roof. The three of them together combine to form a wrecking ball that would put Miley Cyrus to shame. You can take one kid out of the mix, any kid, and the other two will get along like long lost friends. But when all three are together, they get along as well as a honey badger, a hive of wasps, and a wolf with rabies all stuffed into a burlap sack. When it comes to the kids, 1 + 1 = 2. 1 + 1 + 1 = nuclear apocalypse.

Each day of my plate spinning seemed to follow a prescribed routine. The alarm clock on the phone would start screaming. I woke up in a daze, regretting that I stayed up so late watching The Office. I went to work. Aside from occasional trials like trying to unclog a pesky toilet in the patient restroom, I enjoyed my job as a medical social worker.

I drove home from work, occasionally uttering swear words at the people in the fast lane driving 20 miles per hour slower than the speed limit. I made dinner, or cleaned up dinner. I tried to help the kids with some homework. ("Tried" is the operative word here. They are in high school, and their math homework looks more appropriately suited for NASA scientists.) Maybe I'd play the piano for a while. I would feed the dogs. I told the kids "goodnight." Afterward, I would stay up too late watching The Office. Then the cycle would start again the next day.

Life was feeling pretty ordinary and routine. There wasn't anything too difficult or painful. Not that I was complaining. It just made me nervous. I thought, "Things have been going too smoothly for too long." I worried that something bad was waiting around the corner. It seems so insignificant now, but at the time, the most challenging, painful obstacle I faced was a black toenail.

One Saturday afternoon, our family was playing our weekly game of "What activity can we do together that involves the least potential for whining and fighting?" It had been a long time since we went bowling. We talked about a few other possibilities, but this option seemed to have the most interest.

We walked inside the bowling alley and were greeted with torn, dilapidated carpet. In the distance, we heard the sound of one lonely bowling pin being knocked down by a person who was aiming for a strike, but only managed to glance the farthest pin on the left before the ball lurched into the gutter.

After slipping my feet into the chemical-smelling clown shoes, I went to find a ball. I had to quiet my inner germaphobe as I stuck my fingers into ball after glossy ball, trying to find the perfect fit. The light green ball with sparkles, the one that was engraved with the word

"HAMMER" fit my hand perfectly. I have never been interested in joining a bowling league. I have never been invited to join a bowling league. But if my teammates allowed me to adopt the nickname "Hammer," an invite to a bowling league would be difficult to refuse.

I was walking back to our lane when I noticed a jukebox tucked away in the corner. The kids came over when they saw me flipping through songs. Neon letters on the screen of the jukebox said that $10 would buy 17 songs. I saw that the current song on the jukebox was playing loudly on the alley's sound system. I couldn't have pulled my wallet out of my pocket faster if it had just caught fire.

We bought 11 plays in a row of Toto's song "Africa." Then, just for the hell of it, one play of the song "9 To 5" by Dolly Parton. Then 5 more Africas. Then we casually walked back to our lane, trying to be discreet about how many songs had just been credited to the machine. I didn't want any bowlers threatening physical violence toward us once our crime was discovered.

After 8 straight Africas, the employee walked over to the juke box, pushed something on the screen, and skipped Africa. Then he skipped Africa again. It's something that a hundred men or more could ever do. He must have thought he fixed the juke box glitch when the sweet sound of Dolly Parton filled the air. And then it happened. I thought, "I hear the drums echoing tonight." Much to everyone's chagrin, Dolly was immediately followed by the rhythmic drumbeats of Africa. This earned a prompt skip from the employee. Then another skip. Then another skip. It was the most excitement our ordinary lives had seen for quite a while. And we decided that this was the best $10 we've spent in a long, long time.

Later, it was my turn to bowl, so I went over to the rack to get my ball. It slipped out of my hand, and HAMMER torpedoed right into my big toe. I bit my lip to stifle a yelp, and tried to act nonchalant in order to minimize the ridicule from my children. I took my sock off when we got home and saw the damage. It was painful enough that I took a few weeks off from running. The biggest challenge I faced was a sore toe and a few weeks off from running.

That was then. This is now. I long for those ordinary days, back when life was simpler, and there wasn't much excitement beyond working 9 to 5. (Let me pause here for a second, and say how proud I am of myself for managing to tie this back into a Dolly Parton song.) Since then, life has become much more complicated than I prefer. If life had a "Rewind" button, my finger would be pushing it as hard as I could.

THREE

I remember sitting around the kitchen table with old people when I was a kid. The old people were my parents. They were talking with the ancient people, my grandparents. They were lamenting about getting old. They talked about things like multivitamins, pacemakers, and hearing a symphony of crunching and cracking when they bent their knees. My grandpa, who didn't have a single hair to speak of on his head, and deep, grooved wrinkles under his eyes, said "It all started when I turned 40. As soon as I went over the hill, everything started falling apart."

Nothing screams "Epic Thanksgiving Dinner!" like listening to old and ancient people talk about appointments with the cardiologist. I discounted how much legitimacy they were applying to the phrase "over the hill." I knew they must be exaggerating. They were only talking about health ailments because they wanted to avoid a fist fight over politics.

And now here I am at 40, sailing over the hill myself.

I'm coming to understand the meaning of the phrase. "Over the hill" can best be applied to a rollercoaster. You're traveling up the big climb, glancing across the panorama of the theme park, giddy with excitement. Far below, people are playing impossible circus games trying to win a teddy bear, and buying golden brown churros from carts along the street. You hear "click, click, click, click" as the rollercoaster car inches slowly up the hill.

And then the car reaches the peak. The car pauses, ever so briefly, as you are given one final opportunity to take a deep breath.

Then the car speeds down. Straight down. Your stomach slingshots right into your throat, completely preventing any more breathing. Terror burns through your veins. Your body jolts back and forth. As you spin upside down, the safety bar digs into your groin, and you're thankful you had already decided you weren't having any more kids. Your head flies forward, and then slams back into the seat. Then forward, then back. You pray that the chiropractor will have an opening tomorrow morning.

Before my rollercoaster car plunged down the track, I felt invincible. I was athletic and strong. I scoffed at the thought that my ride might get crazy when I went over the hill. But now the car is speeding down the track and giving me a heck of a dose of whiplash. I'll be damned, but my grandpa was right! Everything has started falling apart since my fateful trip over the hill.

With my shirt off, I can see the goosebumps on my arms. The exam room feels so cold that you'd have to chisel a dog off a fire hydrant. The dermatologist walks in and looks like he just graduated from high school. Sure, the scrubs and white coat he is wearing make him look official. But I'm still having a hard time getting over the fact that he was probably writing, "Stay cool, let's hang out this summer," in a yearbook less than three months earlier.

He's doing a routine skin check when he says he wants to remove a small mole on my back. I try focusing on the quiet Eagles song playing in the background to distract me from the injection of the numbing Lidocaine. Right as the chorus of "Hotel California" hits, I feel something drop down the back of my shorts. I think, "Little mole? That thing felt huge! And now I'm going to have to try to fish it out of my underwear."

I look over at his assistant and see her arms start shaking. Short puffs of air escape her nose, like she is making a valiant, but unsuccessful, effort to prevent a laughing attack from overtaking her entire body. I fail to see the humor in a giant mole being scraped off my back and falling into my underwear.

The dermatologist ties a few stitches, and then I put my shirt back on. Once I'm dressed, he says "Can I tell you something?" I brace myself. I know this isn't going to be good. He's going to tell me that the mole is cancerous. "Sure," I say.

"At lunch, I was eating some trail mix. I dropped a peanut, but then I couldn't figure out where it went. When I was taking the mole off your back, I leaned over and the peanut rolled out of my shirt pocket. And now it's in your pants."

Getting a peanut down my pants was only the beginning of a series of uncomfortable visits with people who wear white coats and inflict physical pain for a living.

Lately, I haven't been feeling great. Which is just a tactful way of saying that I have been feeling horrible. For months, my stomach has felt like it is twisted in knots. It has been on permanent spin cycle, churning and groaning like a washing machine stuffed with too many towels. My stomach feels like I've been eating nothing but seven-layer burritos from Taco Bell for months.

I loathe doctors, so I've waited a few months hoping that my TMTBS (Too Much Taco Bell Syndrome) would resolve itself. Unfortunately, it hasn't. Which brings me to an appointment with my primary care doctor, who also happens to be a friend and fellow runner. This is not exactly the kind of magical conversation you want to be having with your physician friend. "Hi. So, um, my stomach feels like I've been eating nothing but seven-layer burritos for the past three months." This conversation is only 1% less awkward than the time I had to do my obligatory "turn your head and cough" exam with him.

I shudder when he recommends a colonoscopy. I wonder which is worse, an enraged Gremlin in my stomach, or a colonoscopy?

A few weeks pass, and then I step up to the counter of the pharmacy. "Welcome to Walgreens. How can I help you?" a man asks with a large smile. I am in absolutely no mood for his cheery disposition. I resist my urge to run away, and instead say, "I need to pick up a prescription for Cory Reese." When he returns with my prescription, he understands my lack of enthusiasm.

He hands me a plastic gallon jug with some white powder in the bottom. "Fill the jug with water, then shake it," he says. "Starting at 6:00

pm, drink an eight-ounce cup of the fluid every fifteen minutes. *And make sure you're not too far away from a toilet."*

I will not go into detail about what happens at my house from the hours of 6:00 pm to 6:00 am. I will tell you two things: 1) Drinking a cup of that solution every fifteen minutes becomes exponentially more difficult as the hours go on. Eventually, just twisting the lid of the bottle triggers a gag reflex. And 2) I legitimately feel that I need to begin a support group called Survivors of Colonoscopies. We could all sit in a circle, talk about the trauma we endured during the bowel prep, hold each other, cry with each other, and try to heal from the horror and shame of that experience.

By the time I start to see sunlight peeking through the blinds, I am utterly exhausted from becoming close, personal friends with my toilet for twelve straight hours. Colonoscopy prep is no crack up, but I knew everything would work out in the end. I did my best to face the challenge with intestinal fortitude.

At the hospital, I barely muster enough strength to change into the overly revealing hospital gown. This degrading wardrobe leaves no part of my anatomy to the imagination. I lay on the gurney and am wheeled into the torture chamber, I mean, operating room.

The lights are dim and it smells like someone just set off a Lysol bomb. The nurse parks me in between a symphony of beeping machines and tubes. Country music is playing quietly in the background. It is awkward to consider that these people standing around me will be listening to Carrie Underwood as they probe around my colon in a few minutes. The doctor comes in and tells me that he is planning to do an endoscopy and a colonoscopy. Essentially, he is planning to stick a tube up my rear, and a tube down my mouth. By this point, I'm too tired to care, as long as he doesn't use the same tube for both procedures.

The colonoscopy doesn't show any abnormalities, so my doctor decides to run a variety of blood tests. The phlebotomist comes to my chair holding so many vials that I want to tell her my body doesn't have that much blood.

At the next appointment, my doctor pulls up the lab results on his computer. I really don't appreciate how solemn he seems. He says "It looks to me like you have something called Common Variable Immunodeficiency Disorder. I'm sorry about these results, but at least now we have some direction to go with treatment." I sit there thinking "Wait. Something in my blood work is making my doctor feel sorry for me? This is way worse than getting a peanut down my pants."

I meet an immunologist who wants to do even more blood work. Then he confirms that I do indeed have Common Variable Immunodeficiency Disorder, or CVID. A common symptom of CVID is the Too Much Taco Bell Syndrome I have been feeling. He explains that, basically, my immune system works as well as a Close Door button in an elevator ... which is to say: not at all.

I only understand a fraction of the medical gibberish that starts coming from his mouth. He tells me that the only treatment for CVID, the only way to strengthen my immune system is to do immunoglobulin infusions. The immunoglobulin is a byproduct of people's plasma donations. He says that the treatment involves sticking three needles into my skin for the infusions. Then he drops the bombshell. I'll need to do these infusions every week. For the rest of my life.

On the outside, I try to look calm and collected, but inside me there is a tsunami of panic. Suddenly I feel nauseous. Fear wraps his burly arms around me and starts to squeeze.

There is one gigantic problem with all this talk about infusions: I am mortified of needles. To me, needles are scarier than snakes, truck stop bathrooms, and Celine Dion music ... combined. I have a bad reputation of passing out when I get my blood drawn. So the idea of being stuck with needles every week for the rest of my life is terrifying.

The medical term for a fear of needles is "Trypanophobia." I find this incredibly aggravating because it doesn't even sound cool. If you're going to have a phobia, at least it could be something with an awesome name, like "Hippopotomonstrosesquipedaliophobia," (a fear of long words), or "Porphyrophobia," (a fear of the color purple). I don't have any idea how or why someone could develop porphyrophobia. But it's no mystery to me why I have a bad case of trypanophobia.

My fear of needles started in college when I had my blood drawn at the local community clinic. The phlebotomist stuck a needle in my vein with only the slightest degree of discomfort. I couldn't even call it pain. Surprisingly, after this little pinch, I thought to myself, "Huh. That's interesting. Everything is getting really dark really quickly." And then I was out cold.

When I started to regain consciousness, my sight came into focus, but for a few seconds I couldn't hear anything. I woke up and didn't know where I was. Two strangers were right in front of my face talking, but I couldn't hear anything they were saying. Eventually, I realized what had happened, and felt embarrassed about my misadventure.

Since that time, I've collected more than my share of embarrassing stories about passing out when needles find their way into my life. It's a horrible feeling. And each time it happens, that link between needles and passing out becomes even stronger.

A nurse shows up at our house on a January afternoon to teach us how to do these dreaded infusions. She assembles all the supplies, fitting all the syringes and tubing together like a jigsaw puzzle. Then she tells me I should alternate where I stick the needles each week. I can stick the needles in my stomach, back, or thighs. I hate how she seems so nonchalant when she says it. She doesn't even flinch when she says I'll be getting needles stuck in my stomach, back, and legs. Every week. For the rest of my life.

"For your first time, let's do your stomach." So I take off my shirt. And I'm sure she is thinking, "Come on, man! Would it kill you to do a pushup every once in a while?" She pokes me with the first needle and it feels like I have a thumbtack jabbed into my stomach. She tapes down the needle that connects to a long, plastic tube where the medicine will flow. After the last two needles are inserted into my skin, she starts a pump and the infusion begins.

The immunoglobulin is a clear fluid, and thick like rubber cement. It feels like battery acid is leaking into my skin when the infusion first starts. But after that, there is only a dull ache. An hour and a half later, the treatment is done. She takes the needles out, and I see little pockets of fluid the size of Milk Duds bubbling up on my stomach.

I've always loved running because of the challenge to overcome obstacles. Every race, every training run, every mile presents an opportunity to keep fighting, even when things get hard. I am willing to suffer because I know it will make me stronger. I am making a choice to suffer.

These needles in my stomach are different. These infusions, these health issues are unchosen suffering. They steal control over how much suffering I'm willing to accept. It's harder to tell yourself, "Don't back down!" when suffering is out of your control.

On the bright side, once I settle into the routine of the weekly infusions, the Too Much Taco Bell Syndrome in my stomach goes away. On the not-so-bright side, the infusions have filled my life with an abnormal degree of suffocating exhaustion. Constantly feeling exhausted is seriously exhausting. Sometimes the fatigue makes life feel heavy and labored, like I'm trying to run in a pool of country gravy. I can imagine that this is how it must feel to be shot with an elephant tranquilizer.

The pockets of viscous immunoglobulin take a few days to dissipate, and they make it too painful to run for a few days after each infusion. With the soreness and exhaustion, I'm not able to train like I used to. Years ago, I fell head over heels in love with running. Imagining my life without running is like imagining The Beatles without Paul McCartney. And yet it feels like these infusions are trying to pry the sport away from me.

FOUR

I recognize that running might not be your thing. If so, I want to change that. I want you to join our gang. I am a huge advocate for the sport, and everything that comes from it. But, admittedly, it can be a little tricky to try and make a sales pitch for why someone should want to lace up a pair of running shoes. Theoretically, people choose various hobbies because they are fun. This point is so important that it bears repeating: people choose hobbies because they are fun. Granted, running can be fun too. But "fun" generally occurs as rarely as a credible sighting of the Loch Ness Monster.

An honest description of running would sound like the television ads for erectile dysfunction medications. The first 10% of the ad is dedicated to what the medicine does, and the last 90% of the ad lists all the possible complications associated with the medication. If there was a television ad for running, it would sound like this:

"Running! It's an exercise that can help you feel just a little less guilty for the three chocolate chip cookies you ate at lunch. (Then the spokesman's voice speeds up.) Warning: running may cause blisters, cramps, sleep deprivation, nausea, vomiting, strained marital relationships, snake bites, sunburns, uncontrollable crying, questioning of one's own sanity, and exorbitantly priced shoe purchases. If you willingly participate in this hobby for more than four hours, see a doctor."

And yet, as miserable as running can sometimes be, I still love it. I really, really love it. Running takes me to a sacred place, untouched by politics, and technology, and screens, and viruses, and hate. It's a place where all you can hear is the sound of your footsteps, and the wind rolling off the top of the mesa. It takes me to a place where I feel peace.

It seems like my health is trying to rob me of this passion. I can feel running slipping away from me, like I'm trying to hold a handful of sand while watching the grains slip between the cracks of my fingers. This is unacceptable. Maybe I'm a few Brady's short of a bunch. Maybe I'm one of those people whose elevator doesn't go all the way to the top floor. But I can't bear to let go of this sport that means so much to me. Sensing that my ability to run is starting to disappear, I need to regain control. Clearly the best way to show my health who is boss is to run a 100 miler.

I'm packing my aid station supplies the night before the Zion 100, and Mel decides that she is going to sign up for the 100k (61 mile) race. "We can run the first part of the race together! It will be fun!" Mel says.

As a social worker, I know many marriage and family therapists. I'd wager that there isn't a single one of them who would recommend running an ultramarathon together as a way to strengthen marital bonds.

On race morning, we hop in the car and make the ten-minute drive to the start line. A horn blows, the race starts, and we promptly begin the adventure with a hideous, abusive climb to the top of Gooseberry Mesa. Including an ascent like this in a race should be illegal, and punishable by law. This little slice of hell climbs around 1,500 feet in one mile. It is vertical, steep, loose dirt. And it is miserable. I would bet my life that there isn't a single runner at the top of the mountain who muttered any less than twelve swear words while making their way to the top. Mel has never climbed this mountain before, and is finding it as pleasurable as getting paper cuts on her eyeballs.

Once we make it to the top, it is finally time to run. Run. Run. Run. Run. Swear. Run. Run. Cramp. Swear. Run. Run. Run. Run. Walk break. Run. Run. Run. Cramp. Swear. Swear. Swear.

After 20 miles of running, cramping, and swearing together, Mel announces that she has now entered the pain cave. Blisters and cramps turn her run into a sluggish hike. The miles begin to pass by in slow motion. I think to myself, "So, this is what a Benadryl overdose looks like." Over the years, she has seen me many, many times in the same condition. Then comes the moment of truth. "Okay, Cory. It's time for you to go up ahead. If you stay with me, you aren't going to make the cutoffs," she says.

I know she is right. We planned to run our own race, and knew we'd split up eventually, but I hate to leave. Eventually, I concede. We give each other a hot, sweaty hug and kiss. It's not the kind of hot, sweaty kiss you read about in a steamy romance novel. It's a hot, sweaty kiss that is covered in salt and smells like a rotting coyote carcass. And with that, I move on.

Over the next 80 miles, I make my way up and down steep, technical trails. I patch a few blisters. I have a few bouts of dry heaving when the Swedish Fish in my stomach decide they want to swim out. There is some shivering and some sleep walking. In the middle of the night, in the middle of the dark, I nearly walk right into a black cow standing in the middle of the trail. Thankfully, I notice the bovine right before my chest meets his rear end. Right at this moment, I am so glad Mel isn't with me. If she had heard my combination of a screech/yelp/whimper, it's entirely possible that she would have filed for divorce right on the spot.

Sometimes I notice discouragement creeping in when I think about how many more miles I still have to go. When that happens, I talk to myself out loud, saying what I'd tell a friend if I was pacing them during a race. "Stop, Cory. Just run the mile you are in."

It takes more than 32 hours, but my scrawny chicken legs finally make it to the finish line. Mel is there to meet me. She fell behind cutoffs and didn't finish the race. There is another hot, sweaty hug and kiss. It's not exactly the kind of romantic kiss that is going to earn us any casting calls for the next 50 Shades of Gray movie.

This finish line feels different than races in the past. I am so thankful I finished before the cutoff. But more than ever, it feels like me and my body are working against each other. We are on separate teams. I would have never imagined I could feel this way. I don't feel like the runner I used to be before starting infusions.

To be a runner, you have to be stubborn. You need to push your limits and not give up when things get hard. You hear your body say, "Okay, I'm tired. Let's go home." But you don't listen. It takes stubbornness to hear that voice, keep going, and then realize that you are capable of more than your body was letting on. I always thought that being stubborn was such a valuable characteristic that helped me keep going when my body wanted to give up.

Like the Zion 100 and many other races in the past, being stubborn and determined is what got me to the finish line. I'm just beginning to realize that being stubborn can also be quite a detriment.

I'm too stubborn to confess my fear that this might be my last finish line. I'm too stubborn to ask for help. I'm too stubborn to admit that my health challenges are leading me into a dark fog of frustration and despair.

FIVE

I am dressed like I'm going to a funeral, which is fitting, because a part of me has died. Mel is wearing a dress, and I'm wearing my nice, blue button-down shirt with a yellow tie. Anytime you meet with the bishop, you need to be wearing your Sunday best.

The bishop is our local congregation leader for The Church of Jesus Christ of Latter-day Saints, commonly referred to as the Mormon church. We only meet with the bishop twice per year. The first visit is the "temple recommend interview." The second visit is "tithing settlement" where we verify that we have contributed 10% of our income to the church throughout the year. The only other reasons someone would schedule an appointment with the bishop is if they want to request emergency financial assistance for something like an overdue utility bill, if someone is seeking spiritual or marital advice, or if they need to confess a sin. But those aren't the reasons we are walking into his office for an appointment.

Mel and I sit down across from the bishop, his large oval desk separating us like a moat. I squeeze my legs tightly together so he won't see them shaking. I've been an active, involved member my entire life. I'm sure the bishop is as shocked at the reason for our visit as we are.

When he asks what brought us to his office tonight, my throat constricts. The words don't want to come out. With a shaky voice, I say, "We've made a really difficult decision. I never imagined I would say something like this, but we've come to a point where we don't believe in the church anymore, and will no longer be attending. We would like to be released from our callings and responsibilities in the church."

The bishop seems taken aback. He tries to talk us out of it. He encourages us to pray, and to think about our family and the eternal consequences that this choice would have. I try to help him see that we have done those things. I tell him that because the church has been such a fundamental part of our lives, we didn't come to this decision lightly.

The drive home is quiet. All the lights are off in the house. It's late. The kids must be asleep. We've been gone longer than we expected. Mel and I walk to our bedroom in numb silence. Her eyes have a glassy look of confusion and detachment. We turn off the light and get into bed. I feel warm tears slide down my face and onto the pillow.

Lying here in the dark, I feel mournful, like I am grieving the death of a loved one. The church has been the bedrock of my entire life. Now, I can feel that foundation crumbling underneath me. And I can feel relentless waves of anguish washing over me. I can't believe how bad it hurts to lose my beliefs. There is no chance I will be able to sleep tonight.

I have dedicated my life to the Mormon church. I have kept all the church's commandments. I have done everything right, and followed all my leader's instructions like a course map that leads to an eternal life with God.

I got baptized at the age of eight, I progressed through the different levels of the youth programs, and was ordained with a priesthood that gave me the power and authority to act in the name of God. I was asked to serve in many leadership positions, and preached about the gospel to others.

Everything we did in church was preparation for the highest possible goal: being able to enter one of the church's holy temples. When I was 19, I met the church's standards and was allowed to participate in the sacred temple ceremonies for the first time.

I was wearing my nicest suit and tie, and was overflowing with a nervous excitement when I passed through the revolving doors at the front of the building. I walked into the lobby where a tall man with hair as white as his shirt, shoes, and suit greeted me with a broad smile. "Welcome to the house of the Lord," he said.

I handed him a small piece of paper the size of a credit card. It is my permission slip to go inside. To obtain this piece of paper, I had a meeting with my bishop, the leader of my local congregation covering the span of a few neighborhoods. He asked me a pre-scripted series of questions to assess my worthiness. He asked if I was paying 10% of my income to the church for tithing, if I kept the Word of Wisdom (no partaking of coffee, tea, or alcohol), if I was honest with others, and if I was sexually pure.

I knew what questions to expect. From the time I was twelve years old, I had annual interviews with my bishop where I was asked the same questions. Thankfully, I passed the test. He issued me the "temple recommend," my authorization to enter the house of the Lord.

Standing in the lobby of the temple, I had no idea what would happen next. My bishop told me that the purpose of my visit was to "receive my endowment." He said that the endowment is a gift from God, but he was not allowed to explain what would take place during this ceremony because it is confidential and sacred. Even though I had spent my life following a course map leading to the temple, I didn't know what was about to happen now that I was finally inside.

My parents had "received their endowment" at the temple. So had their parents. And their parent's parents. Coming from many generations who had been members of the Mormon church, I felt a duty, obligation, and desire to continue the tradition.

After passing the front desk, I was escorted around a partition to the middle of the temple and handed a folded white sheet. Another elderly man dressed in white said, "The first part of your endowment is called the 'washing and anointing ceremony.' Go into the locker room and remove your clothes and underwear, then you can put this shield over you. After you change, I'll take you to a different room for your washing and anointing."

The locker room looks similar to the locker room at a gym, except that it is carpeted. I walked to a small dressing stall inside the locker room. There, I took off all my clothes, and unfolded the white sheet I had been given. It looked like a poncho with a hole on top to slide over my head. It covered the front and back of me, but the sides were gaping wide open. I was mortified at how much of my body was still exposed.

Hesitantly, I opened the door of my small dressing room. It felt like a spotlight was pointing at me. Then I walked through the large locker room, covered only by my shield, as other temple patrons walked by. I tried to not make eye contact with anyone I was passing.

In the room for my washing and anointing ceremony, a different man put a drop of olive oil on the top of my head, nose, lips, and neck. He put his hand underneath my "shield" and put a drop of oil on my back, my chest, my stomach, and my leg. He said that I was now anointed to become a king and priest.

Underneath my shield, the man helped me put on "garments," church-issued underwear. The garments were promised to protect me against Satan, and help provide a constant reminder of my temple covenants. My new underwear looked similar to a white T-shirt, and white cotton boxers that were long enough to go down to my knees.

Although my genitals were never seen or touched, having an elderly man reach under the shield I was wearing and touch my naked body right above my crotch felt incredibly uncomfortable. I shuddered.

I wasn't told what would happen beforehand, and I didn't give consent to be touched by a stranger. But generations of family members had participated in this same ceremony. I thought, "What I'm doing must be okay. Everyone in my family has done this. If there was something wrong, they wouldn't have let me do this."

After my washing and anointing, I went back to my dressing room and was given white pants, white slippers, and a white shirt and tie to put on. Then I was led to the endowment ceremony, a presentation held in a large room with soft, padded chairs facing a movie screen. The ceremony began with a recorded voice playing in the ceiling speakers. An authoritative-sounding man said that I was participating in the ceremony by my own free will and choice. If I wanted to leave the ceremony, this was the time to do so. The voice said that after this point, I would be making sacred promises and obligations. If those promises were ever broken, I would bring upon myself the harsh judgment of God.

Nobody else in the group stood to leave. At the time, it didn't occur to me what was happening. I was agreeing to make promises before even being told what promises I would be making. It was like signing a contract for a timeshare without being able to read the details of the contract first. I had always been taught that this ceremony in the temple was required if I wanted to live with my family forever. The thought of leaving the ceremony never crossed my mind.

In the presentation, we watched a movie about the creation of the earth. Then I was taught special handshakes and passwords that would allow me to return to the presence of God after I die. I made certain promises in exchange for these tokens. I agreed that I would sacrifice everything I have, including my own life if necessary, to support and defend the kingdom of God. I promised that I would avoid any impure or unholy activity. I promised that I would never participate in any sexual activity except with my wife. Finally, I agreed that I would dedicate everything that the Lord has given me, or anything that I might ever be blessed with in the future, to The Church of Jesus Christ of Latter-day Saints.

Before 1990, temple attendees made the actions of penalties, symbolically slitting their throat, tearing out their tongue, or slashing their bowels open if they revealed the secret handshakes and passwords. Because I went to the temple after that time, I didn't receive these specific threats. But it was emphasized over and over the seriousness of keeping the handshakes and passwords a secret. In return for the agreements I made, I was promised exaltation and eternal life with my family.

Going to the temple solidified my commitment to the church. I continued to donate a portion of my income as tithing to the church. Even as poor college students struggling to pay our rent, I still paid 10% of our income because we were promised blessings if we tithed. After we were married, Mel and I wore church-issued underwear which served as a reminder of covenants made in the temple.

I strictly followed the church's regulations to not drink coffee, tea, or alcohol. I read the Book of Mormon. I prayed. I built our entire life on the foundation of the Mormon church. I was a dedicated soldier who could be counted on to help move the church forward. I was all in.

I loved studying the religion's principles and history. I would have never expected that it would be my study of the church's history that would ultimately destroy my faith in The Church of Jesus Christ of Latter-day Saints.

SIX

One night, I sat at my computer doing research for an upcoming lesson I was scheduled to teach at church. I came across a 2014 article from the BBC that started with the line "The Mormon church has said for the first time that its founder Joseph Smith had up to 40 wives." I thought "This must be a misprint." My whole life, I had only been taught about one wife. Then I found an article from the New York Times saying the same thing.

I went to the church's own website to look for information that could dispel this lie. Buried inconspicuously in the Mormon church's website, I found a page labeled "Gospel Topics Essays." The purpose of the essays was to address some of the church's controversial history and doctrines. I had never heard of the essays before this time, as they were never mentioned in any church lessons or conferences. Most members don't know they exist.

There was an essay about polygamy that confirmed the truth of the articles I had just read. I was shocked to learn that one of Joseph Smith's wives was only fourteen years old, and some of the women he married had already been married to other men.

I read the other Gospel Topics Essays and was confronted over and over with troubling aspects of church history that I was never taught. Suddenly, I began to sense a lack of transparency. To me, it looked like a pattern of dishonesty. All my life, church leaders have taught members to avoid anything that contradicts the church's narrative, because those anti-Mormon contradictions are evil. Now, the church was admitting truth to so many things I had previously been told were "anti-Mormon."

The church's essays were like cracking a bookshelf. I had never questioned the church's teachings or restrictions because the Mormon culture was so embedded in my identity, my community, and my relationships with friends and family. There was never a safe space for questions or doubt.

Mel read the essays as well. The more we learned, the more troubled we became. The shelf eventually became so heavy that it broke. It seemed that the teachings about church history were like an iceberg. Leaders taught us the small, glossy part of history that reflected favorably, while hiding the weightier, dark past below the surface. They taught us that we shouldn't look beneath the water, or Satan would seize us. The picture of the church I had been given was incomplete.

Often, church members avoid these uncomfortable topics and contradictions. There is an underlying sense of "I don't want to know too much. I don't want to find anything below the surface that might make me question my beliefs. Because if I no longer believed in the church, my world would shatter."

I understood why the church tells members not to study these questionable issues of church history and doctrine. It felt like coming to the realization that Santa isn't real, while everyone around me is saying he is. Mormons have a strong sense of community. They value prayer, and hold weekly church service. Mormons esteem service. The importance of family is a core tenet of the faith. Members are often known for being reliable, trustworthy, and honest. But just because kids feel good when they get presents from Santa, that good feeling doesn't make him real.

The pattern of dishonesty completely eroded our faith in the church, but we tried to hide our feelings from our friends and family, and continue life as usual. Most of our immediate and extended family, and almost all of our friends are active members of the Mormon church. Leaving the church could put all those relationships in jeopardy. We couldn't bear the thought of breaking those ties.

Members are taught the reasons that someone might leave the church. Either 1) they didn't pray and read the Book of Mormon enough, 2) they didn't have enough faith, 3) they were offended by another church member, or 4) they couldn't live up to the church's strict standards and wanted to sin. As a believing member, I had no idea that, in actuality, the most common reason people leave the Mormon church is because they discover troubling church history and dishonesty.

I know our choice is going to impact relationships with our believing family members, friends, and neighbors. I've seen how church members view apostates. From birth, we are taught that the church makes people happy, and people outside the church can't know true happiness. But we can't continue living a lie. We can't keep dedicating our time, money, and energy. We can't keep pretending we still believe. Which led to our meeting with the bishop.

There wasn't an option to quietly drift away from church attendance. I was in charge of teaching a lesson in the men's group the coming Sunday. I served in a leadership role over the men's group, and was involved in regular meetings. We were scheduled to go to neighbor's houses who hadn't been to church for a while and encourage them to return to regular services. I couldn't bring myself to encourage people to come back to a church that I no longer believed in.

The thing that made our appointment with the bishop so upsetting was the sense of finality. When a loved one is sick, you know the end is coming, but that doesn't make it hurt any less when they pass on. We've come to terms with our decision, in spite of the painful consequences.

I feel like I closed my eyes and stepped off a cliff into the unknown. Nobody ever taught me how to start rebuilding your life after everything you've ever known has been detonated like a bomb.

Two weeks later, I find myself at a store in the mall staring, dumbfounded, at shelves of underwear. I'm glad nobody else is nearby, because a grown man shouldn't look this confused looking at underwear. I pick up various packages, looking at the different designs and styles. I'm going to buy some blue boxers with a pattern of pineapples, just because I can.

A part of me feels like I am committing a sin by buying my own underwear. From the day we were married, Mel and I wore nothing but the church-issued long underwear. The first time we went through the Mormon temple, we were instructed to wear the sacred garments for the rest of our lives so that we could always be reminded of the promises we made, and to always receive protection from Satan. Now here I am, wearing Satan-approved pineapple boxers.

The second equally uncomfortable thing we do is to drink a cup of coffee. Anyone who drank coffee in the church needed to repent of this sin, and was not able to enter the Mormon temple. Until leaving the church, I had never so much as tasted a sip of coffee. It is difficult to disconnect from everything I have been taught, and to realize that drinking coffee is not sinful.

It's difficult to wrap my mind around the fact that two of the most difficult and triumphant challenges that people take to signify leaving the church behind are to drink coffee and wear whatever underwear they want. It is a relief to not have my morality and worthiness based on things like this anymore.

Walt Whitman said to "re-examine all you have been told at school or church or in any book, dismiss whatever insults your own soul." It has taken me 40 years to become brave enough to explore what I actually believe versus what I have been trained to believe.

In most religions, choosing to leave the church means that you simply stop attending. This isn't exactly the case in the Mormon church. When members don't attend weekly church services, they receive calls and visits from neighbors and church leaders. Usually these visits are friendly and cordial, but the underlying purpose of the visit is to encourage those people to come back to church. I know, because I held leadership positions in the church. I was given assignments to make those very same visits.

It is painful to feel a sudden disconnection from our neighbors. Mel and I don't want to lose friendships, but we don't want visits where we are pressured to return to church. We don't want members to encourage us to be obedient and attend services so that we'll be able to see our family in the afterlife. Too many visits and too many comments to us and our children go too far. We want out. The only way to officially leave the church is to submit a formal resignation.

We could have submitted letters to resign from the church, but Mel and I decide to retain an attorney to help us with our resignations. Outsiders might think "Why in the world did you contact an attorney to resign and have your names removed from the church's records?"

Years ago, a guy named Mark Naugle left the church. He found out that there are far fewer stall tactics, and far fewer resignation requests mysteriously getting lost when an attorney is involved.

It just so happens that Mark is an attorney. So he started the website www.quitmormon.com to offer his legal services to others wanting to make the break. For his legal services, Mark's attorney fee is … nothing. He provides his services for free. Mark has helped tens of thousands of people formally resign from the church.

I am surprised that, even with his help, the process is still extensive. Children as young as eight years old are able to be baptized and become members of the church. Before being baptized, children must state that they believe in God, Jesus Christ, and that church founder Joseph Smith was a prophet of God. Yet, at this age, many children still believe in Santa Claus. Lawyers aren't needed to join the church. Photo identification isn't needed to join the church. Notarized documents aren't required to join the church. But with Naugle's attorney services, all those things are required to leave the church. Essentially, it feels like it is easier to cancel a contract with the cable company than to leave the Mormon church.

A part of me feels a tremendous weight lifted now that I'm not surrounded by a culture of guilt and shame. But the other part of me feels heartbroken and demolished. It feels like our family is alone in our own little life raft, surrounded by nothing but an empty ocean.

A friend commented, "It pains me to see that you are taking the easy way out," when he hears about our choice to leave the church. If he understood a fraction of the mourning I feel, the relationships that have been altered, and the pain flowing inside me, he would never say that this is "the easy way."

One comment on the Ex-Mormon Reddit page said, "I think anyone who walks out of the church should walk into a therapist's office." I am starting to understand why. I have just survived an earthquake felt only by me. The wake of destruction is invisible to everyone but myself. I have based my entire life, my relationships, my beliefs, and my faith on the Mormon church. I feel an overwhelming sense of grief now that those beliefs have crumbled.

I hear that most people who leave a religion experience some or all of the Kubler-Ross Model's five stages of grief: Denial, Anger, Bargaining, Depression, and Acceptance. I keep tumbling around those stages like a tennis ball in a clothes dryer. The only stage that continues to elude me is acceptance.

SEVEN

A few months ago I was on a flight to Milwaukee for an ultramarathon. I have always hated flying, but this flight was particularly awful. The person sitting in front of me seemed like he was having a competition with the person sitting behind me to see who could cough the loudest and most often. I just happen to be a Black Belt Germaphobe. The only person who matches my substantial germaphobe tendencies is my wife, who happened to be sitting right next to me.

The three-hour battle of the dual coughers was just the beginning. A few rows up, a child was screaming. The bathroom floor was grabbing my shoes like a sticky mousetrap. Either someone spilled a cup of lemonade in there, or someone had very poor aim. Then we hit some nausea-inducing patches of turbulence. A few times, the plane was dancing around so much that the pilot came on and told the flight attendants to take their seats immediately.

This was my personal hell. There is no possible way this flight could have been any worse. It was the perfect storm with every conceivable airline horror story all hitting at the same time.

My life is feeling the same way, like I've just been catapulted into the perfect storm. A bunch of heavy stuff all hit at the same time. I am discouraged about my health and my dependence on uncomfortable infusions for the rest of my life. I am scared that my ability to run is slipping away from me.

My faith in the Mormon church was the foundational piece at the bottom of my Jenga tower. The church has formed how I act and think. It has shaped my relationships, and the way I see the world. The Church of Jesus Christ of Latter-day Saints has formed the person I am today. That piece has been ripped out, the tower has toppled, and my life feels like a heap of Jenga pieces scattered all over the floor.

I think maybe I could have been able to handle these adversities separately. But having them all assault me at the same time is too much.

The weight of all those challenges has sent me down a path of darkness and the only thing I am is lost.

There's nothing that screams, "For the love of everything holy, DON'T DO IT!" like an obscenely expensive trip to Disneyland with three kids who are far too young to appreciate it, won't remember the trip, who can't go on any of the fun rides, and will whine and fight every single minute they are awake. So, of course, that's exactly what we did when our kids were little.

In the afternoon, we took a momentary break from standing in never-ending lines to watch the parade of Disney characters go by. While we were standing on the side of the street waiting for the parade to start, I wondered which was worse: listening to the kids whine that their legs hurt or sitting on the "It's a Small World" ride while that horrific song burrows its way into your soul.

Once the parade was over, we turned our backs for a few seconds to set up the stroller. And as soon as we went to pick up our youngest daughter Kylee to put her in the stroller, she was gone. We started running in expanding circles trying to find her. It was one of the scariest moments of my life.

We came across an employee and let them know she was missing. The reassuring teenager got on her radio and confirmed that Kylee was waiting for us in the area where parents pick up their lost children. We had to do the walk of shame into a room where a handful of other negligent parents were also picking up their children. We found out that Kylee was so enamored by the characters in the parade that she followed them along the route as the parade passed by, instead of staying by her parents. Apparently, despite their best efforts, parents regularly lose their kids at Disneyland. Kylee was scared to suddenly find herself waiting in a room full of strangers.

Right now, I feel like Kylee must have felt: completely and utterly lost. Life was going well. I was loving the parade. And then, before I really understood what was happening, I got lost. There isn't a colorful room decorated with Disney characters where I can safely wait to be rescued. I'm waiting in the dark, alone.

Nobody is going to come and rescue me though, because nobody knows I'm lost. My smile prevents anyone from knowing what is really going on below the surface. I keep thinking that the fog I'm living in is probably just sadness. Everyone feels sad sometimes. I don't think it's urgent. I just need to give myself some time to sort things out.

The problem is that I keep waiting for things to sort out, but they don't. I feel lost not knowing what to expect with my health. All I know is that each week I feel agitated that I need to do an infusion. I am also angry at myself for what a big baby I am when Mel puts the needles in, and takes them out. Even after doing the infusions for months, they still terrify me.

I am sitting at the kitchen table as Mel disconnects the supplies and starts the process of taking needles out. The kitchen starts spinning like I'm windsurfing inside a tornado. I can feel my skin getting clammy. Beads of sweat collect on my forehead. "Mel, I don't feel good."

Mel is a nurse practitioner. She has been trained to stay focused when situations get tense. She says "Okay, I'm going to hold your hand and I want you to walk over to the couch and lay down."

I know there is no way I'll be able to make it from the kitchen table to the couch in the family room without passing out. I strip off my shirt, and lower myself to the cool tile on the kitchen floor. She patiently waits until the room stops spinning before taking the needles out of my stomach. I am ashamed that I'm such a weakling.

I feel lost about the purpose of my life now that I no longer have the direction and support of the Mormon church. I used to know the meaning of life, but now I'm stuck trying to figure it out on my own.

I have worked so hard to follow the church's rules because their teachings have promised that after we die, we can spend the rest of eternity with our family if we keep all of the commandments. Ever since my dad died when I was a kid, I've been willing to do anything the church tells me to do if it means I will see my dad again. That unshakable belief has shattered, and the pain is unbearable. The darkness around me is becoming increasingly oppressive.

My energy level is nonexistent, and it takes all my will power to get out of bed. I am always tired, yet I somehow struggle to sleep at night. My brain feels like it is being ripped apart at the seams. Searching for a purpose only leaves me feeling lost and empty.

I also feel lost about what to do with running. I am signed up to run the Last Annual Vol State 500k, a 314-mile ultramarathon across Tennessee coming up in a few months. The race is unlike anything I've ever done before. With everything going on, I don't know if I am physically or mentally up to the challenge.

I keep coming back to the fact that, all along, running has been my salvation. It has been my solace and my constant. So many times, running has helped me transform turmoil into peace. Running is a flame that can burn away the shadows.

I don't know if my shadows have become too dark to burn away with a run. They follow me, and wait for me underneath the covers at night. They wait until the lights go out, and it's quiet, and the only company I have is my own thoughts. I am so sick of sharing my bed with them each night. I want the shadows to leave. No, I need the shadows to leave. I can't keep living like this.

Because I'm feeling so much urgency in my search for healing, I decide to attempt the Vol State 500k. I have to hope that a race like this will clear away the fog around me, and show me the light inside myself.

EIGHT

"Once the race starts, which will happen first? Are you going to get bloody nipples, throw up, or are you going to shit your pants?" The race is getting closer, and my friend is genuinely curious. "I don't know," I say. "I hope none of those things happen."

He has an omnipotent smirk painted across his face, like he is looking into a crystal ball. He says "Oh, I assure you, they are all going to happen. It's just a matter of which thing is going to happen first."

For the metrically challenged, the Last Annual Vol State 500 kilometer distance works out to 314 miles. There were two categories to choose from during registration: Crewed (the runner is allowed to have a crew accompany them during the race to provide support), and

Screwed (you get no crew, no aid stations, and you're probably a complete moron.) I wanted to be able to rely on myself, so I chose the Screwed category.

This 314-mile vacation without a car takes runners from Missouri into Kentucky, then across Tennessee, followed by a brief stretch through Alabama, before finally arriving at the finish line in Georgia. The race also happens to take place in July, when temperatures in the previously mentioned states resemble a heat wave in the Sahara Desert.

A lot has changed since I signed up for the race nearly one year ago. I have learned to adapt my training to accommodate my changing health. I'm holding steady physically, although mentally it feels like I am going downhill and can't find the brakes to stop the slide.

But I have faith in the transformative power of running. If a half marathon, or a marathon, or an ultramarathon is good for the soul, running across Tennessee must surely be even better. I can't wait to get out on the course and begin a 314-mile therapy session with myself.

In training, I have tried to toughen up my feet. I've worked on acclimating my body to the impending heat. And most importantly, I've used my training to be able to easily identify discreet places to go to the bathroom when there are no gas stations nearby.

I have a job. I have a wife and kids that I don't want to neglect during training. So there have been many all-night runs while Mel and the kids are asleep. Admittedly, I felt insanely jealous of them in their cozy beds on those nights when I struggled to stay awake on quiet streets. But if it leaves me more prepared, that is a sacrifice I am willing to make.

In the days leading up to the race, I gather the gear I will be taking. My hydration pack is the size of a small backpack. Without any crew members, I need to squeeze everything I might need during 314 miles into that pack, while minimizing weight as much as possible. The pack will carry two liters of water, a reflective vest, blister repair supplies, a toothbrush and toothpaste, an emergency blanket, an external battery and phone charger, toilet paper, a bandana, a travel pillow, a compact jacket, some cash, a poncho, a pocket Mace sprayer, a headlamp, and one extra pair of socks.

I plan to rely on the occasional fast food restaurants and gas stations along the route for food and water. And I expect that I'll stop to sleep only when needed. I'll get momentary rest on the side of the road, or sleep for a few hours in motels. The time limit to complete the race is ten days.

My training time has evaporated. July has arrived. I pack my running gear and prepare to board a metal flying bird headed for Tennessee. My doctor gives me permission to skip my weekly infusion while I am running Vol State. I have no idea if my health will prevent me from finishing the race, but I have to at least try. I need to know that I fought with everything I had.

A pure love of running was the primary reason I signed up for the Vol State 500k nearly one year ago. The race has taken on increased meaning and purpose since then. I am ready to push my limits to the extreme if that's what it takes to find the part of me that has been lost. It is the part of me that knows I am loved, I am whole, and I am enough. I am heading to Tennessee desperately hoping that those 314 miles will unshackle me from the darkness I am being smothered by.

NINE

It's funny what your brain remembers when you combine a fear of imminent destruction with a two hour drive to the airport. I'm sitting in the back seat of Jeff and Carol's SUV, watching the tumbleweeds of Utah blur into the tumbleweeds of Nevada. I'm feeling unsettled and apprehensive, but they seem as calm as cucumbers. We're on our way from southern Utah to Las Vegas to catch our flight.

Sitting in the passenger seat in front of me, Carol looks like the kind of person who exited the birth canal wearing running shoes. She is quiet and thoughtful. Even when she's not saying a word, I can tell that she is constantly thinking. Her brain is a factory that doesn't close.

Carol's muscles look like she could juggle barbells, and crack a Brazil nut between her calves.

Jeff jokes about his lack of training, and says that he is a spokesman for the "Couch to 500k" program. He beams with energy and enthusiasm, and has the ability to create spontaneous friendships with anyone. Jeff has the witty sense of humor of Steve Carell blended with the gentle kindness of PBS painting instructor Bob Ross. He reminds me so much of my dad. From the first time we met, I immediately clicked with Jeff's quirky blend of comedy and happiness.

Jeff and Carol Manwaring ran Vol State together last year. The fact that their marriage endured 314 grueling miles is commendable. They are telling me all the advice they can think of, all the knowledge I'll need to make it from the start line to the finish line. Jeff says "Boudreaux's Butt Paste works best for chaffing." Carol wholeheartedly agrees. Carol says "Make sure to never sit or lay on any grass." Jeff wholeheartedly agrees. Then he tells me about the chigger bites he got last year when he didn't heed that advice. "Those bites itch like hell! They're way, way worse than mosquito bites." Nothing they tell me is comforting. Everything they tell me is revolting.

It has taken ten years from the time I first met Carol and Jeff to this moment where we are driving to Las Vegas, talking about optimal diaper rash ointments. We only live a few minutes away from each other, but we have running to thank for our decade of friendship.

Back then, Carol and I were running marathons, though never together. She was fast, and I was always at the back of the pack trying to avoid an appointment with a coroner. We would occasionally meet up for some group runs on the local trails. I floated to her the idea that

I was considering trying an ultramarathon, and asked if she would be interested in signing up too. She needed no convincing.

So we started running ultramarathons together. More specifically, we ran the same races, but never together. Nothing had changed from our marathon days. She was fast, and I was always at the back with my running partner, the Grim Reaper. Jeff drove to every aid station he could reach to provide support and supplies for Carol.

When I saw Jeff at aid stations, he would find something in his cooler that Carol didn't take when she came through much earlier. (One time he gave me a mid-race feast of fried chicken. Another time, it was a Subway sandwich, and another time it was a cinnamon roll.) We would spend a minute or two dancing the way uncoordinated, middle-aged dads dance (it's not pretty). We would laugh. And then I would be on my way. Later, Jeff ran a few ultras of his own. He was a fellow member of the "Nowhere Near First" club with me.

When they heard about Vol State, they signed up on a whim, and traveled every single one of the 314 miles together. Then, in a temporary lapse of good judgment, they signed up to run the race again. When I told them I had just signed up as well, we planned this carpool to the airport.

Now, we find ourselves looking out the windows of their SUV watching the tumbleweeds pass by. We plan to run our own race. They won't wait for me if I'm on the slow-moving pain train. I won't wait for them if they're in the hurt locker. Everyone hits their highs and lows at different points. It's not reasonable to expect three people to stay together for the whole race. Since I might not see them again once the race starts, I'm so thankful for this pre-race drive to hear their tips.

I haven't booked a return flight. Runners are given ten days to complete the race, but I don't have any idea how many days it will take me. I don't care how many days it takes me. I just want to finish.

TEN

Tennessee's official nickname is the "Volunteer State," where the race derives its name. The only reason "Volunteer State" was chosen for the state nickname is because "Fiery Furnace of Molten Lava State" was too long to fit on t-shirts and mugs. Now we're here, ready to cross the Fiery Furnace of Molten Lava State, and run the Last Annual Vol State 500k.

The sky is as blue as a robin egg when we board a ferry in Kentucky that takes our misfit band of nomads across the Mississippi River. I have never seen a river so grand and expansive. Trees line the banks of the river as it flows like blood inside an artery. Even the Mississippi is in the middle of a race. It follows a 2,350-mile route to its finish line in the

Gulf of Mexico, where the Mississippi meets with the larger body of water and suddenly ceases to be a river.

The ferry takes us across the state line, and drops us off in Missouri. We stand on the shore of Missouri just long enough to watch the race director light a cigarette signaling the beginning of the race. We then get right back on the ferry to cross the mighty Mississippi River back to Kentucky. I love this little idiosyncrasy that allows at least a few steps of the race to be in Missouri.

Once back in Kentucky, groups of runners begin plodding down the back roads and highways of the course. There is bantering, laughing, and stories being swapped. At mile ten, we cross into Tennessee, our third state of the race. Everyone seems to be having fun, while trying valiantly to ignore the heat of the sun crackling like a fireplace directly above us. Maybe if you pretend it isn't there, it will go away.

I am not a stranger to heat. I live in southern Utah, where summer temperatures are regularly hot enough to singe off your eyelashes. But this heat, coupled with the suffocating humidity of Tennessee, is nearly too much to handle. My body feels like it is being tossed and turned inside an industrial-size clothes dryer at the laundromat.

We run upon a string of blacktop threaded through a patchwork of fields radiating green and amber. To the right of us, cars speed by in a hurry to get somewhere. To the left of us, tractors are being piloted by farmers harvesting crops.

In the afternoon, far ahead I see someone sitting on a camp chair in the shade of a highway overpass. When I reach the overpass, I see that it is race director Gary Cantrell, also known as Lazarus Lake. I have no idea how Gary became Lazarus. I think it is part of the mystery. I could ask him, but I think his response would be something like "If I told you, I'd have to kill you, and leave you out here with all the other rotting roadkill." People in the ultrarunning community don't refer to him as Gary or Lazarus. He is Laz.

Laz has a round face, rosy cheeks, and a bushy, greying beard. He looks like the kind of bad department store Santa Claus that kids ask their parents "Was that really Santa?" after sitting on his lap.

The button down white shirt he is wearing fits snug against his stomach. Almost every time I've seen Laz, including at the start line, there has been a cigarette in his mouth. He doesn't look like the kind of person you'd envision taking 126 days to walk across the country. And yet that's exactly what he did a year earlier.

If I didn't know better, I would think that Laz was cryogenically frozen in the Middle Ages when heinous corporal punishment was commonplace, then de-thawed in the 21st century for the purpose of tormenting runners with heinous races. The more insane Laz's race creations are, the more runners sign up for the abuse. Hence, the Vol State 500k fills all openings minutes after race registration opens.

Now, I'm standing here in the shade talking with this living legend of running. My new friends Cherie and Sharon are in the shade of the overpass too. They ask me if I'll take a picture of them with Laz. He puts his arm around each of them for the photo. Then I ask Laz if I can get a quick picture also. He says "Sure, but I'm not putting my arm around you." That is a more than reasonable stipulation.

I walk over and stand next to him. Then, right before the picture, he puts his arm around me. In the photo, I am beaming. And Laz has a bright, cheery smile that any department store Santa would envy.

With a small gaggle of other runners, we stop at occasional gas stations for food and water. Miles tick slowly by, like the hand of a wall clock whose battery is almost dead. We make a brief dinner stop at Taco Bell, just long enough to ingest a few bean burritos and some Mountain Dew. The fireplace we're running in finally cools off a bit when the sun goes down. Our group thins out during the night, some runners moving ahead, and some falling behind on the miles of dark highway.

At mile 38, I see a lighted pavilion ahead where many runners are resting. When I get there, I see my neighbors and carpool companions, Carol and Jeff. They have their shoes off, rubbing their feet. When I sit down next to Jeff, he says "Look at this!" I look over and see his calf twisting and turning like a bag of snakes. I have run many ultramarathons, and I have never seen anything like the cramps and spasms that are convulsing beneath his skin.

Under the pavilion, I take my shoes off and lay on the cement floor so I can prop my feet up on a chair. Moths spin around the crackling fluorescent lights above me. I feel like a deflated balloon. The miles along Tennessee's back roads under a merciless sun have zapped me of my strength and energy. Everything hurts.

I think "If I feel this weary after 38 miles, how is it humanly possible that I will be able to go another 276 miles?" It just doesn't seem possible. I can feel tears welling up in my eyes, but I quickly wipe them away. I can't let anyone see how broken I am feeling, especially considering that we're less than 24 hours into the race. But as quickly as I wipe the tears away, my eyes fill up with water again. One minute later, a runner walks up and says "You doing okay?"

I lie. "Yeah, I'm fine. Thanks."

After resting for a few minutes, I head back out into the night with five other runners, including race veteran Tim Hardy. A few weeks earlier, Tim conducted a conference call where any Vol State rookies could ask questions about what gear to pack, about the course, or about what to expect.

The thing that scared me most during the call was when Tim talked about potential encounters with dogs during the race. "On the back roads, you might come across dogs that can be pretty scary. People have the dogs to protect their property, and the dogs bark like crazy. Most of the time the dogs will keep their distance as long as you keep your distance, and keep moving," he said.

He admitted that a few times, runners have actually been bitten by dogs. This became one of my greatest fears leading up to the race. I desperately hoped I wouldn't come across any mean dogs intent on devouring my tibias.

The five other runners and I pass an occasional street lamp and see an occasional house set back from the road with a glowing porch light. As we begin climbing a steep street, we suddenly hear dogs barking ahead. One minute later, we see three large dogs in the middle of the road ahead of us, barking and growling like a hungry pack of wolves. There is no way around them and the dogs seem determined to not let us pass.

My blood runs cold. We wait for a minute trying to decide what to do, hoping the dogs will back away and let us cross. Instead, their barking becomes even more ferocious. Just then, Tim becomes a determined Army captain, and we become his obedient troops. "Follow me," he says with resolution.

Then Tim does the last thing I would have dared to do: he runs at the dogs. He points right at the dogs, and yells "Go home! You leave us alone!" He runs at them with confidence and authority. "We're not going to hurt you. All we're going to do is pass by. You leave us alone!"

I can't believe what I'm seeing. The dogs continue their unyielding barking, slobber flying from their mouths … but they back up and let us pass by! In the face of fear and insecurity, Tim shows uncompromising determination. He doesn't meekly ask the dogs if we can pass by. He tells them to leave us the hell alone because we're coming through. By showing strength and confidence, even the most aggressive adversaries retreat.

After we're far enough down the road that the barking has stopped, I thank Tim. "Dude. You are the Dog Whisperer! I have no idea what I would have done if you weren't here. There's no way I could have done that if I was by myself."

Tim says "Yeah, you totally could have. When your back is up against a wall, you can't back down. You do whatever you've got to do. You fight back and give everything you've got. Anyone who is brave enough to be doing this race is a fighter."

Over the next few hours, our band of brothers spreads out from each other, and by the time the sun comes up, I am walking the white line on the side of the road by myself. My slow pace allows me to receive an intimate lesson on Tennessee's geography. The course no longer looks like a line snaking across the page of a map. It looks like rumble strips on the side of the highway, and a narrow shoulder, and a cloud of exhaust from the truck that just sped by, and a right turn at the stop sign I see up ahead.

ELEVEN

After twenty-six hours of movement, I walk alone into AJ's All Star Cafe. I sit down and talk with the couple who just got engaged, while trying to keep my eyes from wandering down to the sight of the Maxi Pads taped to the guy's thighs. While I wait for the omelet I ordered, I can feel my pulse beating in my feet.

With each passing hour on day two, the temperature continues to climb. I am a walking slab of buzzard meat. I notice myself inching deeper and deeper into the pain cave. In my mind, I can see the scene in The Wizard of Oz where the Wicked Witch of the West cackles, "I'm mellllltingggg!" as she liquefies into a puddle on the floor. I feel like the Wicked Witch. The heat of day two will provide enough PTSD to fuel many future therapy sessions.

I am scared of running out of water before making it to the next town with a gas station. Because of this fear, I methodically ration my water, which leads to dehydration. During the hottest part of the day, a teenager pulls up next to me in his car. I am alone, and approaching one of those near-desperate moments where I fear that the heat will asphyxiate me. He smiles and says, "Do you want some water?" as he holds up a blue bottle covered with cold bubbles of condensation. With profuse gratitude, I thank him for his kindness. He smiles and says, "God bless you, have a good day." As he pulls away, I start crying. I am so incredibly moved by this small act of kindness.

A few of the vicious degrees on the thermometer begin fading away by late afternoon. After 82 miles, I reach Parkers Crossroads. Traveling on the interstate, you might blink and miss it. But a 30-minute-per-mile pace caused by a day in an industrial clothes drier makes the road through Parkers Crossroads feel like I might never cross through to the other side of town.

I must be hungry. I can feel my stomach growling. But the idea of actually eating anything feels reprehensible. I walk into a Subway restaurant to order a sandwich. As I am waiting in line, my stomach decides to go into complete revolt. I am on the brink of vomiting. I desperately want to avoid a Technicolor yawn in the middle of the restaurant while other customers are standing around me.

Finally, it is my turn. I step up to the counter, imagining that my face must be turning as green as the sliced cucumbers sitting in their little black tray in front of me. "Can I please get a foot-long tuna sandwich on wheat?" When the word "tuna" leaves my lips, my stomach clenches and quivers like in a slow motion movie where a guy gets hit in the gut with a cannonball. My stomach screams, "Damnit, Cory! Tuna?! Tuna?! What in the actual hell are you thinking?"

Once the sandwich is made, I stand at the register. "Would you like any…" I say "No" before she can even say "chips with that?"

"Would you like any…" I say "No" before she can say "cookies?"

I swipe my debit card and dart out the door. I feel so overwhelmingly proud of myself for making it through that entire transaction while keeping my stomach from erupting.

I walk to the side of the building, away from the restaurant parking lot, where only the truck drivers at the gas station next door might be able to see me. And then my stomach begins seizing and purging out everything that is inside. Which is … nothing. I stand there for a few minutes dry heaving, wiping tears from my eyes while sweat drips from my forehead. Then I keep moving down the road, tuna sandwich in hand.

My body is begging for rest after not sleeping for more than 40 hours. The stagnant heat, combined with the sleep deprivation, have demolished me. I decide to check into a motel to sleep for a few hours. Usually, when someone is renting a cheap motel for only a few hours, something bad is about to happen. This is no exception.

A warm breeze hits me when I open the door, and I choke on the overpowering smell of musty armpits. There must have been another runner who slept here for a few hours before I checked in. A bedspread has been hastily pulled up over the dirty sheets. And that was the extent of the "cleaning" between me and the previous occupant. There are no towels and no soap or shampoo in the bathroom. But what the room lacks in hygiene products, it more than makes up for with hair. Hair covers the sink and bed. The shower is so furry that it looks like its wearing a mink coat. The previous occupant might have very well been a Labrador Retriever.

I sit down on the bedspread that has surely been in this room since 1972, and take off my shoes. My heart sinks. Large blisters have formed, and my feet are looking angry. I force down a few bites of my tuna sandwich, stomach be damned. Then I tiptoe to the shower, trying to avoid aggravating the painful pockets of fluid on my feet. I make a pathetic attempt to dry off with a washcloth, and curl into the bed. I am so tired that I don't care if the sheets are hairy and smell like a kitty litter box.

90 minutes later, I am jolted awake with the beeping of the alarm on my phone. I do my best to wipe the sleep out of my eyes, and dig out the first aid kit that has been nestled deep inside my hydration pack. Then I let a safety pin go hog wild on my blisters. That relieves some of the pressure, but my feet still feel tender and broken.

More than a hunger for food, I am hungering for connection. My friends from home, my carpool companions, are somewhere out here on the course. I miss their company, and I know being with them could make a world of difference. I don't want to be out on the road during the night alone. So I text Jeff and Carol to see where they are on the course. They are approaching Parkers Crossroads, so I tell them I will wait and meet up with them. I also tell them to avoid ordering a tuna sandwich at Subway if they know what is good for them. After spending most of the day alone, I can't wait to meet up with them as we tackle the second night of the race.

We meet up in the lobby of McDonald's and then head back into the Tennessee abyss. We fill the hours laughing about past race experiences, watch owls sitting on telephone poles hooting at the moon, and listen to Brené Brown's Netflix special, all in an effort to keep ourselves awake. It's now around 3:00 a.m., and our conversation has slowed. There are more gaps of silence between people talking. We all confess that we are sleep walking, dozing off mid-stride. "Maybe we should take a 20-minute power nap," Carol suggests. I can't agree fast enough.

We find a quiet pad of cement far off the side of the road that looks like a heavenly place to sleep. We lie down on the asphalt, using our hydration packs for pillows. As my body hits the ground, the asphalt and my hydration pack pillow are as comfortable as the most luxurious hotel bed I have ever slept in. The pack forms perfectly into the bend of my neck. The warm summer air covers me like a soft, down blanket. We laugh at the roaring symphony of crickets and croaking frogs that have come to sing us a lullaby.

We look up at a canopy of one million stars. They look like snowflakes close enough to grab and squeeze into a snowball. I see them aligned in constellations like a road map in the sky, pointing the way to go. Right at this moment, lying on the asphalt underneath a galaxy of stars, I am overwhelmed with an engulfing sense of peace.

Even though the air is warm and muggy, this feeling of serenity gives me chills. My arms and legs are covered with goosebumps. It's the same sensation I used to feel during spiritual experiences at church. Watching the stars spread across the heavens like glitter, I am having a spiritual awakening. Going into the race, I wouldn't have guessed that it could become a religious experience.

I don't want to forget how I'm feeling right now. I don't want this to end. I wish I could inhale this serenity and never exhale. In the moonlight, I can see a small, white pebble sitting next to me. I reach over and put it in my pocket. I'll keep it with me for the rest of the race. When times get tough, it can remind me of this pervasive peace.

Twenty minutes later, our tranquil slumber ends, and we're back to the road. I dread the faint light crawling over the horizon as we ease into day three of this journey. The instant the sun sneaks over the horizon, we are enveloped in its flames. By this point, it is becoming more difficult to excavate stories that are funny or interesting enough to distract from the glowing ball of fire in the sky. Our mantra has become, "Just get to Parsons. Just get to Parsons."

Parsons has gas stations and fast food restaurants. Because Jeff and Carol ran the race last year, they had an idea of where they would be each day. They have a motel room reserved and waiting for them in Parsons where they plan to get a few hours of afternoon sleep. I call the same motel to see if there is a room available for me to rent. I hide my sense of defeat when the front desk clerk says, "Sorry, we're all sold out."

When we reach Parsons, I see a towering church across the street from Jeff and Carol's motel. Sleep has become like an assassin who snuck up behind me, threw a thick, black garbage bag over my head, and is patiently waiting until I stop moving. I have no doubt that under the shade of the church, I will be sound asleep within three minutes. We plan to sleep four hours through the worst heat of the afternoon, then meet up again and continue down the road.

I walk behind the church and sit against its wall to take my shoes off. I am glad Jeff and Carol aren't with me because of the involuntary whimper that slips out of my mouth as I cautiously remove my socks. I lie down on the shaded cement, eager to slip into a race-induced coma, when my phone begins ringing. It is Jeff. "Hey. Our room has two beds! Come and sleep over here."

I resist. I don't want to impose or make the situation awkward. "That's so nice of you, but I'm just fine out here. Seriously, don't worry about it."

"It's not an option," Jeff says. "Come over here, or I'll come and get you."

I know he'd do it. I slide my shoes on and walk across the street. I wipe my eyes before I knock on the door. I don't want them to know that I have been crying on the way over to their room because of their act of kindness. When the door opens, cold air floats from the air conditioner to welcome me and delicately caress my skin. The room feels like walking into the refrigerated foods section at Costco.

As they sort through their gear, I sit down on the spare bed and remove my shoes and socks again. Then I notice my knees. Despite periodically applying sunscreen, my knees are bright red and covered in tiny pockets of pus that look like soap bubbles in a kitchen sink. Tennessee's roads are doing their best to cremate me before I'm even dead.

The wreckage of my sunburn is child's play compared to the wreckage between my legs. Chaffing and a violent heat rash have incinerated everything from my knees up to my waist. Yes, unfortunately everything. Radiating heat from the road has created dark, weeping welts on my thighs. It looks like I sat down for a naked picnic on top of a hive of fire ants. I get a pit in my stomach and think "Uh oh. I'm in big, big trouble." With jolts of agony pulsing through my crotch, I can't help but ask myself, "Why do bad things happen to good people?" The crotch region is just about the very last place you'd want pulsing with agony.

With limited room in my pack, I didn't have space for extra clothes. The only shorts and shirt I have for the race are the shorts and shirt I am wearing. After a few days in the Tennessee furnace, my clothes are covered in sweat, and as stiff as a sheet of drywall. "We found out during the race last year that it's best to wash your clothes out and let them dry while you take a nap," Jeff says.

I doubt my friends want any mid-race nudity after inviting me to stay in their room. I tell him that I didn't bring any extra clothes, so I will rinse my clothes out, hang them up to dry, and wrap a towel around myself to sleep in the bed next to them.

Jeff says "If you want, I have some extra underwear I haven't used yet. You're welcome to wear them to bed."

I have heard the phrase, "A true friend would give you the shirt off their back." I would like to file a formal request that this phrase be modified to, "A true friend would give you the clean underwear out of their pack." Did I take Jeff up on his offer? You better believe it. After I maneuver myself into and out of the shower, then hobble back to my bed, we all sit there in our underwear comparing our grotesque, puffy blisters. I know that it is time for me to sleep when I begin to hallucinate Dionne Warwick standing near the motel desk singing, "That's What Friends Are For."

TWELVE

I listen as Jeff and Carol talk about the upcoming stretch of the course we will be tackling when we wake up in four hours. My eyelids are being weighted down with sandbags and they refuse to stay open. I curl up in my bed. I am living in a lap of luxury: a blowing air conditioner, a fluffy pillow, and sheets as soft as a baby unicorn. Not to mention some blissfully clean underwear. Life could not be better. I am certain I'll be asleep faster than you can say, "Fruit of the Loom."

Jeff and Carol lay down too, and within minutes I can hear heavy breathing as sleep overcomes them. I am beyond exhausted, but sleep refuses to come across the room to pay me a visit in my bed. It feels like I have dumped a bucket of sulfuric acid onto my lap. The deep, raw sores that cover my thighs and groin from heat rash and chaffing are so painful that it takes my breath away.

I curl up in fetal position and clench my jaw. I don't want moans of agony to leave my mouth and wake my roommates. I am immersed in colossal discouragement knowing that my sores are extensive enough that they will not be able to heal anytime soon. These sores are going to be accompanying me for the rest of the race.

I doze off for 20 minutes before the piercing pain wakes me up again. I just want to buy a pack of cigarettes and go smoke away my sorrows in the motel bathroom. I have never smoked a cigarette in my life, but this seems like as good a time as any to start.

Rage burns inside me knowing that despite my soul-crushing fatigue, the alarm will be going off soon and we will be returning to that thin shoulder on the side of the road. "If only I had some Maxi Pads I could tape to my thighs," I think.

When the alarm goes off, I walk over to the rack where my clothes are drying. Thanks to Tennessee's thick humidity, my clothes are still completely soaked. If legs could talk, mine would say "You're joking, right? You can't seriously plan on wrapping us up again with those wet shorts? You thought your chaffing was bad before? You ain't seen nothing yet kid!"

I come out of the bathroom and hand Jeff his underwear. He doesn't put them in his pack. He puts them right on. My pre-Vol State brain would have said, "Friends don't let friends swap underwear." But my mid-Vol State brain doesn't give this odd transaction a second thought. In the midst of a 314-mile battle like this, swapping underwear doesn't even register on the radar of insanely bizarre things.

After laying down for a few hours, the muscles in my legs have twisted into pretzels. It takes significant coaxing to get my legs to walk out the door of the motel. On the horizon, thick purple clouds are concealing the sun. The wind smells like rain. I check the weather app on my phone to see if the storm is heading our way. The radar projection on my screen looks like a tie dye shirt splashed with green, yellow, orange, and red. The wet clothes we just put on aren't going to be drying out anytime soon.

A few miles pass before a laser light show of lightning cracks across the sky. A rolling drumbeat of thunder sounds like a growling dog on the other side of a chain link fence. And then a fury of rain cascades from the purple clouds. We dart into the open bay of a car wash to put our ponchos on. Within minutes, the street gutters are overflowing as torrents of water pour down. We have already spent many hours in a motel and don't want to waste more time twiddling our thumbs in the car wash waiting for the storm to pass. So, armed with our $1.00 plastic ponchos from Walmart, we hesitantly leave the comfort of the car wash and enter the flash flood.

Storms come and go for the rest of the night. A $1.00 Walmart poncho can only protect you from the rain so much. We still get wet, but wet clothes aren't the worst thing that comes from a storm. When I think rotting roadkill couldn't possibly smell worse, rain on a hot road proves me wrong.

So far, we have come across an immeasurable amount of roadkill on the side of the road. We have gotten to know the smell of roadkill before we even see the lifeless animal. Skunks smell terrible. Possums smell terrible. Deer smell terrible. But the absolute worst smelling roadkill corpses are the armadillos. They smell like a combination of a clogged gas station toilet, moldy cheese, rotten eggs, sweaty armpits, bad breath, and vomit.

I lament my bloodhound-like sense of smell. Of all five senses, the sense of smell is the absolute worst one to have as my strength. That pungent smell of roadkill has become locked in my nostrils. I can smell the odor, whether a dead animal is around or not.

At 11:00 a.m. on day four, we slog into the town of Hohenwald at mile 144. After dodging rotting armadillos all night, we are desperate for a shower and beds. I walk into the lobby of a motel that smells like burnt toast from an earlier continental breakfast. Carol goes to sit down on a fuzzy pink chair while I stagger up to the check-in desk. "Hi, do you have a room with two beds we can rent?" Hohenwald isn't exactly a booming metropolis, so I figure this shouldn't be too much of a problem. Exhaustion has left my emotions fragile. I can feel my eyes getting moist when the clerk says, "Yeah, we've got one but we need to finish cleaning it, so it will be about a half hour."

I don't need the room in a half hour. I don't need the room in five minutes. I need the room, and my shoes off, and the shower, and the bed, right this very second. We have no other options. I turn around to tell Carol the bad news. But she is already sound asleep on the fuzzy pink chair, her chin nuzzled softly on her chest. "Okay," I say. "We'll take it." I sit down on the other fuzzy pink chair in the motel lobby. The next thing I know, the guy from the front desk is standing next to me with some plastic room keys saying "Cory, your room is ready."

We sleep away the heat of the afternoon and are rudely awoken five hours later by a screeching alarm clock. We select our dinner stop one mile up the road at Taco Bell. Standing at the counter ordering my food, I look behind me and see that Jeff is surrounded by a group of people.

After ordering, I walk over to see what the commotion is about. He is getting the same amount of attention from people that Taylor Swift would get if she walked into Taco Bell and ordered a chicken taco combo meal.

People seem fascinated by this group of runners passing through their town. They are full of questions for him. The Vol State race has become well-known in Tennessee. The communities we pass through are fascinated and intrigued (and possibly disturbed) by these athletes who show up to run across their state. (I use the term "run" VERY, VERY loosely. By day two, most "runners" are lucky to manage a shuffle.)

It's as if the communities are voluntarily becoming "road angels." There are no aid stations in this race. There is no official assistance. But there have been so many small gestures of kindness during our trip, so many people who have found joy in giving us encouragement. That has been the case even if we are sitting at a table stinking up the dining area of a Taco Bell. It feels like these road angels seem to show up at the times when I am feeling my lowest, and I am desperate for some human connection.

One night, we were out on a desolate stretch of road. A truck stopped ahead of us and a man got out. "You guys are awesome!" he said. "I have some cold fruit cups here in a cooler. Do you want something?"

Another night, I walked into a gas station feeling bad because I was getting the floor wet. I was dripping from the torrential downpour we were walking through. I got up to the counter with a bag of peanuts and a bottle of Gatorade. The clerk said, "It's on me." He refused to let me swipe my debit card.

One morning, the sun had just come up and my skin felt like I was laying on a rusty barbeque grill. I was scared I was going to run out of water. Then we came around the corner and saw a shaded canopy next to the road ahead. When we arrived, we met a lady named Sue. She had a cooler of ice, soda, and water. She had sandwiches and the most incredible damn pasta salad that has ever entered my mouth. It was an exquisite masterpiece. The cucumber chunks. The olives. The feta cheese. The sweet, red cherry tomatoes. The red peppers. The green peppers. And Sue didn't stop there. She dug deep and even included yellow peppers! Every purposeful ingredient was held together with a dressing so delicious that it must have been imported directly from Italy. "Sue. This pasta salad is seriously incredible! Did you make the Italian dressing? It tastes amazing!" Sue laughed. "No, honey. I just opened a bottle of Kraft dressing and dumped it on the pasta."

These are only a fraction of the many, many road angels we have seen. There have also been so many unseen road angels. I can't count how many people have had a little table with snacks or a cooler of drinks in their front yard for runners who pass by. It is the fourth night, and we find ourselves in a rural area, struggling to make it to the top of a steep hill. We are sore, hungry, and sluggish from fatigue. We can see a porch light at the top of the hill, and it becomes our goal to make it to that light.

It is past midnight when we get to the top. Once there, we see that a canopy has been set up in the front yard, along with three camp chairs. Carol, Jeff, and I collapse into the chairs. There is an audible groan of relief from each of us. We eat some granola bars from a box sitting next to the chairs. Then we open a cooler that is placed next to the box of snacks. A can of Mountain Dew instantaneously vanishes into my throat.

There is also an enormous bottle of pickles inside the cooler. It is one of the industrial, gallon-sized jars. It's the kind of bottle you see on the counter of gas stations. And, of course, that bottle in the gas station is always completely full of pickles. Because anyone in their right mind is not going to walk into a gas station, see that bottle of pickles covered in six years of dust, and say "You know what I need in my life right now? One of those humongous pickles." The pickles inside those gallon jars are the size of muscular kangaroo femurs. One pickle is so enormous that it could feed a family of five for at least three days.

Jeff says "Those pickles actually look kind of good."

I can feel a surprised look cross my face. "Seriously?"

Jeff seems to be surprised that I am surprised. "Yeah, I'm going to eat one." He sticks his hand into the narrow mouth of the jar and starts fishing for a pickle, the same way you would stick your line through a hole into the water if you were ice fishing. He catches a fish, I mean pickle, and takes a bite. "Dude. This is so good. Try one!" I can't deny the fact that I am starving, so I go fishing too.

It turns out that the pickle does taste so good! Jeff eats another pickle. Then I eat another pickle. Then Jeff eats another pickle. Then I eat another pickle. The only reason we eat six pickles between the two of us is because that's all the pickles that are left in the bottle. I shudder to think how many more we would have tried to stuff into our stomachs if there had been any more pickles. When life gives you lemons, thank life for the gift, then kindly ask if you can exchange the lemons for some pickles.

More than any other time in my life, I am noticing the kindness of strangers. So many times during the race, I have thought to myself, "People are so, so good." While out on this long road across Tennessee, I wonder how many opportunities I've missed to be a road angel back at home.

THIRTEEN

We are required to use our phones to log onto a website and check in with our current mileage at 7:00 a.m. and 7:00 p.m. each day. Our check-in link also has a space where a comment can be written about our current state of affairs. Scrolling through other runner's comments gives us a guaranteed laugh twice each day. Some of our favorite check-in comments are:

- "At the store, the clerk says, 'Have a nice day.' My only truthful response was, 'No thanks, I have other plans.'"
- "Just when you think you're dead, you're able to walk a 55 minute mile."
- "Hang in there, it will get better. Sorry, I lied."

- "I rented a hotel room by the hour and left my underwear behind. What have I become?"
- "I went to a gas station in Shelbyville and there was a guy standing outside with a 6-pack of beer. He said he would give it to me for free if I touched him inappropriately. There are some SICK people in this world. Anyway, I would love it if some of you could catch up. This beer is getting heavy."
- "I'm talking shit way more than I ever have in my life. Also, that has a completely different meaning than it did a few days ago."

While I have my phone on to do my check-in, I see a post on Facebook from Laz. I can imagine him sitting on a camp chair, sleep deprived from the stress of directing the race. There's probably a cigarette in his mouth. I can imagine him nodding off as he types his own race update to share with the world. I'm thankful for the time he put into his update, because his words are just the inspiration I need right now:

a hundred private wars
while the world watches the magnificent battles being waged up
 front,
a hundred private wars are taking place on the back roads of
 tennessee.
most of the warriors who are out there will never be famous.
stories will not be told about their exploits,
except among the family that is the vol state runners.
they are not elite athletes,
just regular people like you and me.

but they have a hunger that drives them.

a need to find the greatness that is inside each of us.

something that compels them to step on that ferry,

on an ordinary day in july,

and to set off on an impossible quest.

today they are completely absorbed in a great battle.

the battle between their body and their mind.

running 314 miles is every bit as hard as it sounds.

the muscles ache

the feet cry out in pain.

there are sunburn and blisters

hunger and thirst.

bleary, sleepless eyes that long to close.

sometimes there is loneliness

sometimes despair.

314 miles sounded doable at home.

314 miles sounds like an impossible dream

alone on the side of some godforsaken road,

with a body that has already performed the impossible.

and surely can have nothing left to give.

days to go before they can set aside their pack and shoes,

and the compelling need to move onward

to finally rest the unsullied rest of the victor.

they have chosen this rocky path

over ease and comfort.

and now they must summon the will to continue

when their body cries for relief.

when escape is only a phone call away.

the world may never know their name.
but on this day
they will find in themselves
a strength they never knew was there.
the greatness that is in each of us,
if we have the will to call on it.
it is what they have come to find.
and that is the prize they will take home.
yes, these are just ordinary people.
engaged in a hundred private wars.
but out there on the open road,
they are accomplishing extraordinary things.
Laz

We make it to Columbia, Tennessee on day five. Again, we try our best to avoid being out on the road during the hottest part of the day. We check into a motel room, and plan to take a quick shower, then sleep for a few hours. My shoes and socks give just the slightest bit of cushion against my blisters. When I try to walk barefoot from my bed to the bathroom for a shower, the pain is unbearable. It feels like walking on shards of glass. I drop to my knees and crawl to the bathroom. I am a pitiful sight. I can't stand in the shower. I have to sit down and let the water fall on me.

I am discouraged by how much effort it takes just to get out of the shower. I get dressed and crawl on my hands and knees back to my bed. We are 175 miles into the race, and every cell of my body feels defeated. I knew this race would strip down all my defenses, and reveal a raw vulnerability, but I never expected I would feel quite this raw.

In the evening, we set out on the road again. The night is pitch black by the time we reach a worn, red bench sitting in front of a convenience store. This distinctive monument is known as the Bench of Despair. Laz said The Bench of Despair is "one of the most well-known landmarks on the Vol State course. Located only slightly past the halfway point at mile 186, this resting spot comes when most runners hit their low point ... realizing that the end is still so far away. The bench offers nothing more than a quiet place to rest, and an overwhelming realization that there is still a lot more suffering to come."

A few obligatory pictures with the bench later, we're back to the pavement. My body has become an Ambien pill with legs. The fatigue is relentless. As difficult as the miles are on my body, the effect of sleep deprivation is proving to be equally debilitating.

We can only go a few miles past the bench before we are all ready to collapse. In my mind, three words are playing on repeat: Need. Sleep. NOW. We find a post office and peer through the windows into the dark lobby. Prayers are answered when we tug on the door and find that it's unlocked. Using our hydration packs for pillows, we lay on the post office floor. It couldn't be more comfortable if it were a down feather mattress. I fall asleep within five breaths. Suddenly, I'm no longer in Tennessee. I am magically teleported to Costa Rica.

FOURTEEN

Our nap is only 20 minutes, but I slip into a dream that makes me feel like I've slept for hours. For some reason, my dream carries me back to a vacation earlier in the year to Costa Rica.

After arriving at the airport, Mel and I were shuttled to the resort by a kind Costa Rican man who serenaded us while showing off that he knew every word to the Richard Marx song playing on the radio. I didn't want to be the jerk who said, "Dude, this isn't something you should be bragging about." We walked into our room at the Planet Hollywood Resort. Above the television was a quote by Ferris Bueller emblazoned on the wall: "Life moves pretty fast. If you don't stop and look around once in a while, you could miss it."

While lounging in the pool, we saw some swimmers holding their hands up in the air with their thumbs touching and their index fingers pointed up in the air forming the shape of a U. I wondered what they were doing, and asked one of the employees who was in the pool, also with his fingers up. He said "This is how you catch dragonflies!" He must have seen the confused look on my face. "Well, you don't actually catch them. This is how you get a dragonfly to land on your fingertip. We call it 'catching a dragonfly.'"

At first I thought he was joking. I had never heard of anything like this before. So I decided to go ask a little girl who was doing the same thing. She told me she was catching dragonflies! I said, "I've seen you holding your fingers up for a long time. Have you caught any yet?" A smile of pride flashed on her face as she said, "Yeah, I've caught a bunch of them. Try it. Just hold really still with your fingers up and you can catch some too. Your arms will get tired, but keep them up and hold still."

I noticed that there were lots of dragonflies flying around the pool. It was at that moment that I made an ultimatum: I refuse to leave Costa Rica without first catching a dragonfly. I made a U with my fingers and held them high in the air. I stood there watching, waiting, anticipating that at any moment a dragonfly was going to land on my fingertip. Then my arms started getting tired. The little girl was right. I kept waiting and waiting. I tried to hold still. And yet … nothing. I'm sure it reflects on my absolute lack of muscle mass in my arms, but I couldn't keep my arms up nearly as long as the little girl next to me.

I tried catching a dragonfly the next day. And the day after that. My success rate was exactly 0%. When it was time to fly home, I had to concede that I was leaving Costa Rica without achieving my goal.

A few months later, I was reading an article online that mentioned the figurative meaning of dragonflies. These winged insects often symbolize transformation and hope. I learned that they live most of their lives as nymphs, and are only able to fly for a short amount of time. Because of this, dragonflies are a reminder to live life to the fullest because we only have a short amount of time to be here.

Reading the article about dragonflies, I immediately thought back to my time in the pool and the experience took on new meaning. The little girl told me that holding my arms up would be hard and I would want to quit, but to not give up. And if you don't give up when it gets hard, you'll find hope and transformation in the form of a dragonfly.

At 1:00 a.m., the alarms on our phones begin their obnoxious orchestrations together, waking me from my dream. Our nap is over and I'm back in Tennessee. It was nice while it lasted. But now it's time to get back on the road. I can't give up. I need to keep pushing and let the race transform me.

FIFTEEN

We stumble back into the night looking like the Three Musketeers if they had been buried alive, and just barely managed to claw their way out of their graves. When you're stone cold drunk on sleep deprivation, emotions can become raw. You'll find yourself sobbing with laughter at things a fully functional person probably wouldn't think are mildly amusing.

You might notice getting irritable about trivial things, or find yourself having difficulties with simple tasks like ordering food. You could end up standing in a McDonald's staring at the board of food options, and thinking, "I'm too tired to even decide what I want to eat." Keeping up with conversations can be highly challenging. Simple math equations are virtually impossible. "We're at mile 201, and the race is 314 miles long. How many more miles do we have to go?" Figuring out such a question is akin to understanding the theory of relativity.

Sometimes, the effects of sleep deprivation are funny. But most of the time, sleep deprivation is absolutely debilitating. Those times can be very dark, both literally and metaphorically. I become more acutely aware of all the other physical ailments I'm facing. I start questioning why in the world I would willingly participate in something like this when I could be sitting on my couch at home eating ice cream and watching a movie.

When I run 100-mile races, night is always the most challenging time for me. Fatigue feels like a blanket wrapped tight around my face trying to suffocate me. That feeling is multiplied exponentially during Vol State. Our three-person team is working to keep each other engaged and focused as a means of holding back the sleep monsters as much as possible.

In the pre-dawn hours of day six, we make it to Rock Market near Lewisburg, Tennessee. Even though it is only 4:00 a.m., the grill inside the gas station is open and taking orders. We each order a BLT sandwich, then lay on the floor of the gas station resting our feet for the five minutes it takes to prepare the sandwiches. We start to notice the absurdity of our situation, lying on a gas station floor at 4:00 a.m. waiting for sandwiches, and we start giggling. Then the giggles morph into a complete outburst of laughter. We are laughing so hard that we are crying. We could be arrested for public intoxication, and we would fail the sobriety test of walking a straight line. Except that instead of being drunk on alcohol, we are drunk on exhaustion. I am thankful that in this moment of pure misery, we are still able to howl with laughter like inebriated baboons.

An angry sun is blazing across the sky by the time we make it to Lewisburg. We are now six days, and 201 miles into the race. My feet are in severe distress. Blisters are covering the bottoms and sides of my feet, and between my toes. Every step sends volts of electricity shooting up my legs.

I have had plenty of experience treating blisters in the past, but past experience is no match for the destruction of Vol State. I began giving birth to blisters on day two. I use the words "giving birth" because eventually the blisters were big enough to need birth certificates. If given the option between having these blisters or being catapulted through the third-story bedroom window of Oprah Winfrey, I'd take the catapult.

The heat radiating from the road is like a toaster oven. I have no doubt that if I put a pepperoni Hot Pocket in each of my shoes, I could set the shoes on the road for three minutes and then have myself a fully baked lunch. Between the scorching heat, and the fact that my feet are always wet from sweating, my blisters have quickly gone from bad to worse. My blisters never get a chance to heal because I am constantly in forward motion.

The frustrating thing about blisters is that, even after being popped, they often refill with fluid. Before checking into our motel in Lewisburg, I stop at Walgreens to purchase a sewing kit. I learned about a trick for blister care where a needle and thread can be inserted through the blister. The key is to leave a piece of thread sticking out of the blister. That way, the hole doesn't seal completely, and the fluid can wick out.

I go to work on my feet, and become quite the little seamstress, sewing and patching my blisters.

On the seventh day, we get caught in another flash flood, followed by a heat wave of smothering humidity once the storm blows away. We get caught in the heat of the day with no shade or cloud cover, and we struggle immensely. This is a quick way to lose 15 pounds of sweat within one hour. My skin is withering like a dry raisin.

I lost my hat somewhere along the way. Maybe I accidentally left it behind in a motel room. I need a hat to keep the sun out of my eyes, but the hat selection is limited at the gas station where we stop. The best option is a bedazzled denim hat with the word BOY written in plastic jewels across the front, and glowing plastic jewels covering the brim. It's not pretty, but it will get the job done.

That evening, we stop at a Subway restaurant in the city of Manchester, mile 250 of the race. Before ordering my food, I walk into the bathroom and see myself in the mirror. I look like I have just been jumped into a gang. Everything, everything hurts.

I don't want to waste any time, so I sew while I eat. Take a bite of my foot-long tuna sandwich on wheat, then pop a blister. Take another bite of my foot-long tuna sandwich on wheat, then pop another blister. Once we start moving again, I am filled with dread. My feet are in worse condition than ever. All the doctoring I have done hasn't made my feet feel any better. The blisters are gnawing at my feet like a pack of hungry dogs. "Leave me alone, go home!" I want to yell.

As we're walking, Carol tells me that she has lots of experience fixing blisters. She offers to work on my feet. Initially, I decline. I hate that I have let myself reach such a poor condition. I have already taken advantage of wearing her husband's underwear. I don't want to impose even more by getting help with blisters. But my feet are at a crisis point. I can't keep going like this.

Eventually, I relent. I lay down on the cement of a car dealership and gently remove my shoes and socks. I watch moths flickering in the fluorescent lights above us. Jeff takes a 20-minute power nap next to a Toyota Corolla while Carol tries to mend the damage inflicted on my feet by that merciless, unending Tennessee road. When we resume movement, my feet feel a little better. I desperately hope they will be able to hold up long enough to travel the last 64 miles of the race.

Sixteen

During the night, I think about those 20 minutes laying on the cement of the car dealership. That was an opportunity for me to learn an important life lesson. I hate asking for help from others. I don't want to depend on anyone else. But, as Carol was draining blisters and taping hot spots on my feet, I had this lightbulb moment. I thought about how it's okay to ask for help. In life, people are eager and willing to help if you're willing to let your walls down and stop being so stubborn. This might be an easy concept for other people to understand, but I am stubborn. I couldn't see it until now. Each passing day of the race strips away more of my defenses, like peeling away the layers of a moldy onion.

I have been running, walking, and slogging for exactly one week straight by the time we begin the steep climb up to the city of Monteagle at mile 273. One solid week of forward motion. Thick forests of trees line both sides of the winding road. After a hefty supply of sweat and swear words, we make it to Monteagle. We rest at a motel for a few hours before putting our shoes back on to keep going. It is 6:00 p.m. and we are going to walk across the street from the hotel to grab dinner at the Mountain Goat Market. Once I put my shoes on, I encounter a distressing problem.

I. Simply. Can. Not. Walk.

My feet are a flaming pile of wreckage. Every step feels like hundreds of needles spiking through the bottom of my feet. I am not considering dropping out of the race, but I have absolutely no idea how I will be able to even make it across the street, let alone another 40 miles.

The three most dreaded letters in an ultrarunner's vocabulary are DNF. Those three letters next to someone's name on the race results infer an unaccomplished goal. Did Not Finish. I've come so far in this journey. I've worked so hard. I simply don't know how I can keep going, but I know I don't want a DNF next to my name. I've always believed in the importance of finishing what you've started, but now confidence is leaking out of my body with the beads of sweat.

Carol sees my fear and concern. "Here, let me help you," she says. Again, I have no other options. I sit down on some stairs outside the market while Jeff goes inside to order food. My arm rests on my leg when I bend down to take my shoes off. I can feel the pebble from earlier in the race inside my pocket. Now, more than ever, I am desperate to feel some peace.

We sit in silence as Carol works on popping and patching blisters. I quietly start sobbing. Normally I'm not an overly emotional person. But out here, I can't help it. I'm seeing a different side of myself. I can't fathom that my feet could possibly hurt so bad. I feel embarrassed about the desperate state I am in. I hate feeling so helpless. And I am overcome with profound gratitude for her kindness. I can't remember the last time I cried so hard. Carol is focused on my feet, and I try to conceal my overflowing emotions.

Then she looks up and sees my tears. The expression on her face remains stoic and focused, but I see heavy tears filling her eyes. We have built such a powerful bond of empathy and love. As she works, everything around me blurs. I don't feel the wind blowing the leaves on the bush next to me. I don't hear the cars driving by. All I notice is the warmth of Carol's empathy. She is feeling my pain with me.

In this moment of being supremely broken, I now recognize life's meaning with pristine clarity. We are here to endure. We are here to be a beacon of light in the darkness. We are here to help others turn hurt into healing. We are here to spread hope, and radiate love.

Eventually, Carol repairs my feet enough to keep going. I don't think she did anything different with my feet than I had been doing, but the simple act of tenderness lessened my pain. She will never know how much her compassion means to me. We all sit at one of the tables in the market, each of us choking back tears while we eat our dinner. I'm sure the people around us are wondering how chicken pesto sandwiches could make someone so emotional. We resolve that from this moment on, we're going to push as hard as we can. It's time to get this thing done.

We all battle the desire to pull off on the side of the road and go to sleep, but in the middle of the night, we witness a surreal experience. Amidst the thick forest of trees bordering the road, we become enshrouded in thick fog while lightning bugs blink like strands of Christmas lights all around us. It is an occasion of pure magic, and feels as if we are walking right through the set of a Steven Spielberg movie.

During the race, it has seemed like we were constantly being barraged with unique and difficult challenges that we had to figure out and overcome. Sometimes we would just shake our heads, smile, and think, "Is this really happening?" Sometimes we would say to each other, "This is another one of those experiences that we'll probably look back on and laugh." When times got ugly, we only had two coping strategies: either start laughing or start crying.

With three miles left until the finish line I hear a choir of angels rejoicing as the heavens open up to celebrate our finish. I am completely flattered that heaven is weeping tears of joy on our final stretch of the race. Heaven is weeping heavy, pounding, relentless tears of joy, accompanied by lightning in the distance, and roaring thunder above. Then heaven starts weeping harder, and harder, and harder. We are swallowed by a flash flood so powerful that I wouldn't be surprised to see the sky raining actual cats and actual dogs.

The final miles lead us through a maze of dirt roads lined by fields of corn. With the sky hemorrhaging water, the dirt roads have become streams. The downpour seems so incredibly appropriate. It is like Vol State wanted to give a final reminder to say, "Wow, you've been through some shit. You've faced a lot of hard things out here and you didn't give up. You would have been perfectly justified to quit, but you didn't. When the sun beat down, and when the sky let loose its fury, you faced the challenge and you kept fighting. Cory, you are stronger than you know. When life tries to beat down on you and lets loose its fury, I hope you remember this."

Ever since we met up at a McDonald's on night two, I have spent every minute of the rest of the race with Jeff and Carol. Over the course of this 314-mile trial by fire, they have seen every good, bad, and ugly side of me. I can tell they love me even more because of it. I have seen their good, bad, and ugly sides, and I feel the same way.

We weave back and forth through a path of trees while the rain beats down. Then the trail opens up in a clearing and I see a large rock ahead of me that signifies the journey's end. When we get there, we each bend down and kiss the rock. Laz has been there at the finish line waiting. He stands up from his camp chair to congratulate us. He asks about my hat, and I say, "I lost my hat a few days ago, so I had to buy another one at a gas station. This was the best they had."

He laughs, and in his southern drawl says, "I love it. That is the spirit of Vol State. When you meet a challenge, you improvise, adapt, and overcome." He can't know how much I respect him and how much this sentiment means to me. I want to hug him, but I know I shouldn't. I am soaking wet, and have the aroma of a rotting armadillo.

Then Laz says, "Normally I don't want to get anywhere near you runners at the finish line because you smell so bad. But we should swap and get a picture wearing each other's hats." I put on his hat, and he puts on mine. Then he puts his arm around me, and I get a photo at the finish line with Laz wearing a hat that says BOY written out with large plastic jewels.

It has taken eight days and six hours to get here. I can't believe that I am finally standing at the finish line with my friends. I hug Carol and

Jeff. We have come to know each other's weaknesses, fears, and insecurities.

I say "Thank you guys so much. Thank you for sharing motel rooms with me, and telling me stories to keep me awake when I started sleep walking, and helping me with my blisters. I'm so thankful for the time we've spent together out here."

They tell me that the race worked out just how it needed to, and that I helped them just as much as they helped me. It's nice of them to say that, but I know it's not true. I never loaned either of them a pair of underwear.

We escape the rain, and spend some time under a canopy, watching a few other runners arrive at the finish line looking like cats who have just been sprayed by a garden hose. Then we drive to the closest motel to stay for the night. Carol says, "We might as well continue our week-long streak, and share a room tonight."

Jeff and Carol are planning to stay in Tennessee for a few more days, but I buy a ticket to fly back home the next day. Once in the room, I take off my shoes and moan. My feet are wrinkly from hours of rain, and angry as a nest of murder hornets. Again, I resort to crawling from my bed to the bathroom.

"I don't think I'm going to be able to put my shoes back on tomorrow," I say. "I have no idea how in the world I'm going to walk through the airport to get to my terminal."

While I'm in the shower, Jeff, whose feet have fared better than mine, drives to a Walmart across the street. He returns with some leather slippers, and says, "Here. You can wear these at the airport." These slippers are not going to transform me into a runway fashion model. They look like the same slippers my grandpa wears. But they will definitely be more comfortable than my shoes. I might be able to make my flight after all. Jeff is the epitome of the kind of road angels our world needs.

I could feel something changing in me during that race. Hard, crusted layers of me were peeled away. I was left feeling vulnerable and raw. While out on the course, I didn't have a spare ounce of energy to expend on depression. My only focus was to make forward progress. All the outside noise was quieted.

We sit in the motel room eating pizza, laughing, crying, and talking about what a wild ride we've been on for the past eight-and-a-half days. All the walls I had built up around me were broken down, mile by mile. We are talking about our favorite memories of the race, when I notice myself saying something that I don't think I would have said 314 miles ago.

"It's hard to top that feeling of making it to the finish line, but I think the most meaningful part of the race for me was at mile 273 when my feet were hurting so bad, and you took off my shoes and helped bandage my blisters." I look over at Carol and say, "I hate asking for help, and I hate crying and showing my emotions. That was really hard for me to do, but I felt so much better afterward."

I don't tell them that I've always had a hard time exposing my thoughts and feelings. They don't know that I've always struggled asking for help. I also don't tell them about the dark fog of despair that has been surrounding me during the months leading up to the race. I just sit here on the worn motel bedspread, eating pizza, and thinking about how nice it feels to have some of that darkness fade away.

SEVENTEEN

I consider asking for a wheelchair to help me get through the airport to my gate, but decide to make the expedition by foot. Despite my Walmart grandpa slippers, the mere act of walking requires a herculean effort. The blisters are sending a dazzling meteoroid of pain with each step, and my knees are achy and stiff. For the incredible experience I had during the Vol State 500k, I don't resent the discomfort one bit.

It takes weeks before I can walk without feeling like I am stepping on cactus barbs. For a few weeks, I wake up in the middle of the night, panicked that it is time to leave the motel room and get back on the road. Each time, I feel overwhelming relief when I come to my senses and realize I am in my own bed and can go back to sleep.

I catch myself thinking about the race day and night. Memories keep popping up that must have been repressed as a result of sleep deprivation. A few nights ago, I was trying to fall asleep when I remembered that I ate mid-race beef stew from a gas station. I don't know how I had forgotten this experience, and I don't know why it suddenly popped into my brain at 11:30 p.m. when I was waiting for some sheep to show up that I could count. But it did.

Immediately, I was right back on the road. The morning sun. The humidity. The tiny beads of sweat on my arms. My calves trying to seize up with cramps after 232 miles. Jeff says, "There's a little town called Wartrace right up the road. They have a gas station, so we can get something to eat there."

Thirty minutes later, we walk inside the Wartrace Country Store. I feel as happy as a dog with two tails. I realize that at this stop, I won't need to resort to my usual mid-race gas station purchase of a Butterfinger, a bag of Fritos, and a bottle of Dr. Pepper. Nestled at the back of the store, past the rows of candy bars, sunflower seeds, and Twinkies, the country store has a grill! Up until now in the race, I've consumed so many Butterfingers, Fritos, and bottles of Dr. Pepper that they don't even sound good anymore.

The special for the day is beef stew. Now, in a normal frame of mind, unclouded by sleep deprivation and lasers shooting through my feet, I probably wouldn't have considered eating gas station beef stew. But right now, I am in the middle of Vol State. And I would sell my pancreas for a meal that isn't pre-packaged high fructose corn syrup, dextrose, and maltodextrin.

The potatoes in the gas station stew are tender and flavorful. The carrots are soft and sweet. The meat is, well, meaty. We sit in a little booth eating our stew out of Styrofoam bowls, watching customers walk in and out of the store, and raving about how you couldn't find better food at a five-star restaurant. It's memories like this that keep me up at night.

In the weeks and months following Vol State, I think back on the most difficult times of the race, the times when my feet hurt the worst, and the times when sleep deprivation was physically painful. When I was at my lowest points, I genuinely don't know how I was able to keep going.

As I settle back into regular life, I can feel a fog of sadness begin following me around again like a stalker hiding in the shadows. It's naive to think, but I really hoped that my time in Tennessee would permanently clear out the storm clouds. The clouds cleared momentarily during the race when it took every ounce of energy to simply survive. Even though I was often in pain, I felt happy and fulfilled. It was bliss. In Tennessee, the exhaustion was so all-consuming that even depression couldn't manage to wedge itself inside me.

A grueling 314-mile ultramarathon is a pretty extreme measure to take in hopes of defeating depression. It is ignorant to expect that pushing your limits to the extreme will guarantee endless, healing peace in your heart. And yet, that's exactly how I treated the race.

I hoped that Vol State would dismantle me like a Russian nesting doll. Each adversity I faced would remove the outer layer of the painted wooden doll, getting me closer and closer to my true, happy self after each challenge. At the very least, I figured a steady diet of Butterfingers and Fritos would be a potent antidepressant.

But depression didn't decide to break up our relationship and stay in Tennessee. It didn't wave goodbye and yell, "It's been nice knowing you!" when I boarded the plane to come home. The darkness I felt before the race is still here after the race.

We have a Great Dane named Little Debbie who is like a 165-pound shadow. She follows us from room to room. If we go into the bathroom, she will walk in too. If we kick her out and lock the door, she will sit outside the door whining, waiting to be reunited again. If we are in the kitchen making dinner, Debbie will lay on the cold, hard tile next to us instead of going to lay on the soft carpet in the front room. She is always there, refusing to leave our side.

Winston Churchill said he felt like his depressed mood followed him around like a black dog. It is a description that anyone with a four-legged friend can easily recognize. I am noticing that depression has become like Little Debbie, an obnoxious companion that refuses to leave me alone.

Even after Vol State, I can feel the dark fog waiting for me when I wake up in the morning. It follows me around all day. And when I get into bed at night, it lays down on the carpet next to me, curled right up against the night stand. Then it patiently waits for me until I wake up so that it can follow me around again.

Sometimes I can temporarily lock it out of the room. I might be doing something fun with my family or friends. Sometimes, I go on a run, or sit down to play the piano, or dive into a good book, and the darkness will momentarily clear. But depression is never far away. It always waits patiently right outside the door, anxious to resume being my 165-pound shadow as soon as the door is opened.

Much to my dismay, I realize that you can't outrun depression.

EIGHTEEN

Every morning, I stand in front of two sliding glass doors. The doors sense movement and roll open with a hum as they glide on their tracks. My nose catches the faint scent of Clorox and chemicals. I walk past the chairs in the lobby, down the hall, past the dietitian's office, and into a large, wide open room of dialysis patients. Each person sits reclined in a vinyl chair, connected to a machine. Throughout the day, I sit with them. We talk about their lives, their hopes and fears, their health, their jobs, their families, and the challenges they face as a result of their kidneys not working. My dialysis patients are like teachers.

There is palpable vulnerability as they sit in their assigned chair for many hours while a machine cleans their blood. They will need to have a dialysis treatment every other day for the rest of their lives. Seeing my patients so often, we get to know each other well. My patients offer a unique perspective on life because of their health challenges. I find myself constantly surrounded by valuable life lessons.

As a medical social worker, a decent chunk of each day is spent charting notes into a computer. I also make a lot of phone calls to coordinate insurance coverage, which leads to long periods of time sitting on hold listening to agonizing flute solos. (Utah Medicaid Office, I'm looking at you.) But my favorite part of the job is the face to face talks with people during their treatments.

On a Monday afternoon, I sit on a chair across from one of my patients. She has two big needles in her arm. One tube is carrying blood from her body to a dialysis machine, and then another tube is returning the bright red blood back to her body. An occasional alarm beeps on the nearby dialysis machines signaling that someone's blood pressure is too low or too high.

A nurse is doing an assessment on the patient a few chairs away. I try to tune out the commotion around me as I talk with my patient. During my conversation with this 68-year-old woman, we talk about her health and the difficulties she is having adjusting to a new life on dialysis. That adjustment, and the sudden lack of independence and control, is often tough to manage.

Right in the middle of our conversation, I hear the Sir Mix-a-Lot song "Baby Got Back" begin playing on someone's phone. The synopsis of this 1992 hit is that Sir Mix-a-Lot likes big butts, for which he cannot lie. The ring tone gets to the lyrics "Cause I'm long, and strong, and I'm down to get the friction on," before she reaches into her purse, touches her phone, and the song stops.

I am so taken off guard, and can't wrap my head around how this song was coming from the phone of my sweet 68-year-old patient. It's not exactly the kind of anthem you'd expect to be endorsed by someone who qualifies for a senior discount at Kentucky Fried Chicken. We finish our conversation, and I move on to the next patient. But I can't shake what I've just experienced.

The next time she is at the dialysis center, I pull up a chair next to her. I feel awkward asking the question to someone who is old enough to be my mom, but I sheepishly say, "Hey Vivian, was that your phone that was playing 'Baby Got Back' last time I was here?"

She giggles like a teenager and tells me that it was her phone. "Being on dialysis sucks," she says. "Sometimes you just need a good laugh. Every time my phone rings, I hear that song and it makes me smile."

Sometimes I like reading self-help books. I've learned a lot of strategies for building happiness. But not one of those books has suggested the simple and effective intervention of changing your ringtone to "Baby Got Back." When life gets hard, sometimes you need to dig deep for little things that can bring joy.

Another morning, I sit across from a patient in the middle of his dialysis treatment. Since the time he began dialysis four years earlier, I have never seen this 86-year-old man smile. Admittedly, I can understand why. His body is still paying the price for his many years of service in the military. Every conversation I have with him revolves around his failing health and his loss of independence. But today's conversation is particularly harsh.

He tells me that because of poor vision and general weakness, he isn't able to drive anymore. A decent chunk of his limited income goes to paying for transportation to dialysis. Walking is difficult, and he faces constant exhaustion. Small tasks like making lunch are a challenge. He has to provide care for his wife when he barely has the energy to care for himself. He has to sleep sitting up in a recliner because if he lays down, he has difficulty breathing. With gruff frustration, he tells me how discouraging it is that he can't even sleep next to his wife anymore.

I am at a loss for words. The social worker side of me wants to help make the situation better and provide some relief for his burden. But I just can't think of anything that could make it better. I grapple for how to help.

We talk about how to cope with chronic illness and how to better utilize the support network around him. We talk about taking advantage of the days he feels good and how to work through the days he doesn't feel good.

I do my best to empathize and provide a listening ear, and try to allow him permission to release some of the steam that has been building up. After some time, I can sense that emotions have simmered down. He seems to be in a slightly better frame of mind.

Our conversation comes to a close. As I stand to leave, I say, "Thanks Gene, it was good to talk to you."

He mutters back "No, it wasn't."

I sit back down. I look at his tired eyes and say, "Gene, it really was good to talk to you. When I drive home from work tonight, I'll be thinking of this conversation. It will remind me how lucky I am to have independence. I'll probably go for a run tonight. If I do, I'll try to remember to be thankful that, for right now, my legs can run down a trail. When I go to bed tonight, I'll see my wife next to me. I'll think about our talk, and I'll feel grateful for something so simple as being able to sleep in a bed next to her. Talking with you helped remind me to enjoy the little things, because you never know when they may be taken away. I really need to work on not taking things for granted. Our talk helped me a lot. Thanks."

I stood to leave, and said "Gene, it was really good talking with you." He reached over and grabbed my hand. Then I witnessed something I never thought I'd see: Gene smiled.

Sometimes I get frustrated with myself. At work, I am given keys to strengthen happiness. I am constantly reminded to appreciate the simple things, and live in the moment. And yet I still find myself being led away from those things when feelings of discouragement or busyness creep into my life. I can learn a lot if I really take the time to listen to the wisdom all around me.

NINETEEN

Help is not coming.

Vol State is not the only sadistic race devised by Lazarus Lake. He also concocted the Barkley Marathons, one of the most tortuous 100-milers in the world. Since its inception, only fifteen people have finished the race.

Tennessee's Brushy Mountain State Penitentiary was a maximum security prison for the worst of the worst criminals, including Martin Luther King Jr.'s assassin, James Earl Ray. Somehow, Ray managed to escape from the prison in 1977, but was then met with brutally steep mountains covered with painful briars and thorns. He could only cover eight miles of the punishing terrain before being caught 55 hours later.

Scoffing at those eight measly miles, Laz figured he could cover 100. And thus, the Barkley Marathons race was born. Each year, Laz comes up with a unique 20-mile loop that runners must complete five times. Most runners argue that the loops are closer to the 26-mile marathon distance, especially accounting for all the times they get lost.

And why do they get lost? Because the course isn't marked. You aren't allowed to have a GPS watch. All you get are a map, a compass, and condolences on your stupidity. You'd have to climb Mt. Everest twice to equal the race's 60,000 feet of elevation gain. There are no aid stations, no volunteers, and absolutely no mercy.

The race's motto is emblazoned on the bib of every runner crazy enough to attempt Barkley: help is not coming. It is an explicit warning that every runner accepts. Don't depend on anyone for anything. Whatever food and water you might need, you carry yourself. If you fall down and hurt yourself, you stand back up and keep going. If you get lost, you're in charge of finding your way out. You can't rely on anyone because you are entirely, mercilessly on your own. You are in charge of figuring your shit out.

This is precisely the way so many people approach depression, including myself. I am on my own. There is no one who can help me. I'm not going to come across an aid station full of gummy bears and Coke to help me feel better. I am off course, lonesome, and gut wrenchingly lost. And the only one who can help myself is me.

I'm trying to find my way out of the darkness on my own, but I just keep feeling more and more lost. It's like my mind is so weary and numb that I can't tell north from south on a compass.

I never fully understood depression until I experienced it myself. While I was working on a degree in psychology, I learned a lot about depression. (I also managed to get bit by a rat. During one psychology class, we were given an assignment to use a reward system to teach our rat to push a bar in his cage. My rat preferred gnawing on fingertips instead of pushing a bar.)

Then I moved to Laramie, Wyoming for graduate school. In my Masters-level social work classes, we made a deep dive into understanding depression. Each teacher had a wealth of experience, not only as a professor, but also as a therapist. They knew what it was like to sit across from someone in crisis. They taught us what depression looks like, and what depression feels like. They showed us how to identify depression, and taught us about the many different ways that depression can be treated. By the time I had a Master's degree a few years later, I felt confident in my understanding of depression.

I started working as a therapist as soon as I graduated. I was comfortable walking into the dark with people. Over the course of a few decades, I got better and better at helping people work through depression. I understood depression from a clinical perspective. But understanding depression from a clinical perspective is vastly different from understanding it intrinsically and intimately.

In my high school physics class, our teacher said he was going to teach us about the rods and cones inside our eyes. Standing in front of the class, he showed us a series of cards with colorful numbers, and asked us to write down what number we saw as he went through each card.

After going through all the cards, he reviewed the answers. He said, "Okay, on the first card, you'll see the number sixteen. But someone with colorblindness would see the number seven." I looked down at my response and saw the number seven. "On the next card, you probably wrote down the number five. But if you were colorblind, you would see the number twelve." I looked down. Twelve.

With a pit in my stomach, I raised my hand. "I don't understand. All my answers say I'm colorblind, but I can still see colors." He said that people with normal color vision might be able to see up to one million different colors and shades and tones. But someone with colorblindness might only see 10,000 to 20,000 colors and shades, only one or two percent of the normal range.

Last year I heard about EnChroma glasses, specifically designed to help people with colorblindness see more colors. I bought a pair as a birthday present to myself.

When the glasses arrived, I went outside, closed my eyes, and put the glasses on. I opened my eyes, and suddenly saw shades of reds, greens, and blues that I didn't know existed. The world immediately had more depth and brilliance.

I could have listened to people explain the different shades of reds, and greens, and blues. But until I saw those many shades of colors for myself, there is no way I could have fully understood. It is the same with depression. Now, my comprehension of depression goes beyond a textbook explanation. I more fully understand it because I am experiencing it.

A few years ago, Mel and I spent our anniversary in Iceland. Over the course of nine days, we drove the Ring Road, an 821-mile road circling the entire country. We ate horrifically expensive food. ("Are you *sure* that hotdog costs $40.00?") We stayed at horrifically expensive hostels. ("No, I guess I don't mind sharing my bathroom with six other European hippies.") And we saw the most stunning vistas, mountains, and waterfalls in the entire world. We had just visited Dynjandi, a waterfall hours away from the beaten path of the Ring Road. White ribbons of water cascaded down the mountain creating a rainbow that arched across the sky.

On our way back to the hostel, we drove a steep road through the Westfjords of Iceland. Our rental car struggled to maintain speed as the road kept climbing higher. Within minutes, our car was engulfed in a thick cloud of fog. We could only see a few feet ahead and behind us. Our muscles tightened as our visibility decreased. We didn't know if we were about to run into a car driving ahead of us, or if we were driving on the edge of a steep mountain cliff. "I'm scared," Mel said, in between her tears. "I know. I'm scared too," I said. A black cloud surrounded us, and we didn't know how to get out.

My whole life, I have felt so content and fulfilled. But between coping with my new health challenges, and stepping away from our religious beliefs, I suddenly feel myself suspended within a black cloud like the one I saw in Iceland. Light has drained out of me, and I am only a shell of myself. I am the living dead.

One night, I am standing at the bathroom sink washing my hands. I look at an impostor staring back at me in the mirror. All I see is emptiness. There is no gleam of life in his eyes. There is no enthusiasm or energy. There is no purpose. I see dark bags underneath his hollow eyes. Then I have such a surreal thought, "I do not recognize that person looking back at me in the mirror." The fog is building. I am standing in front of a stranger.

Henry Rollins said, "It's sad when someone you know becomes someone you knew." I am experiencing that loss.

I miss me. I used to have a spark. I used to have clarity, and warmth, and ambition. I used to be alive.

TWENTY

The days are blurring into weeks, the weeks blurring into months. I don't really know who I am anymore. I can't reconcile "this me" with the "old me." I used to be so driven, so full of energy. Now I am completely empty, a room with all the furniture removed, and the blinds closed tight. I can't stop the fog from continuing to thicken all around me. The only things I am capable of feeling are helpless and alone.

My thinking is clouded. I am discouraged that nothing I am doing helps me feel better. I am angry at my unending fatigue. I can't keep living like this. I am stuck in the dark and the stars are refusing to shine.

It is a Tuesday night and I have to wake up early the next day for a meeting. I am indescribably tired. I want to tell Mel that I am in a bad place. I need some help. As we're getting ready for bed, I try to talk, but the words get lodged in my throat and refuse to come out. I know she would help me. She would do anything for me. But I don't have a single cell of courage to tell her how weak I am. I hate that I can't bring myself to say anything.

We get into bed and Mel quickly falls asleep. I toss and turn for more than an hour, but sleep alludes me. I stare at the ceiling as the minutes of another hour tick by. I wonder how many others are staring at a ceiling right now, facing a sleepless night with a brain that won't turn off. The inability to sleep, and the suffocating darkness, leave me feeling powerless against the despair.

I reach over to the nightstand and grab my phone. When I turn it on, an eerie, blue light illuminates the dark, making my bedroom look like the chamber of a haunted house. Thankfully, the light doesn't wake Mel up. Even though she is lying right next to me, I am thoroughly alone. And then I do something that surprises and scares me. In the Google search bar, I type "ways to commit suicide."

My finger is shaking as I touch the phone screen. The moment I click the search button, a deafening fire alarm begins wailing in my head. I'm the only one who can hear the alarm. I'm in trouble. My depression just crossed a line. Hearing that alarm, I suddenly grasp just how low I am, and just how desperate I am feeling. It's not exactly that I want to die. I'm just not sure I want to be alive.

I burst into tears as I realize how much I am hurting. It is a rare moment of self-compassion. If I could give myself a hug, I would. I feel so saddened that I have arrived at this point. I don't want my life to end with a DNF, the devastating Did Not Finish.

When you're exhausted in the middle of an ultramarathon, a DNF sounds so appealing. The lure of dropping out is intense as you desperately crave rest, and a reprieve from the pain. You think, "It doesn't matter whether I finish or not. Nobody cares if I drop out." If you are able to persevere and finish the race, you're glad that you didn't DNF. But in the moment of suffering, it's hard to think that far into the future.

I turn off the phone. The neon blue glow on the ceiling dissolves into black. I don't know how I am going to feel better, but at least I have enough insight to realize that this isn't the solution. I am caught off guard. It is terrifying to see how depression can warp your mind, and make you think things that would never have crossed your mind before. Darkness took control of my mind. After so long trying to resist, I almost became too tired to fight back.

The scary thing is that this isn't the first time I've felt the hot breath of suicide breathing down my neck.

When I was a kid, my basketball was smooth and slick, thanks to countless hours of shooting hoops in the driveway. When we got home from school, my younger brother and I would play for hours. Then, when my dad got home from work, he'd play with us for a few more hours. The basketball court was our favorite place to talk about our day. It was a classroom where life lessons were taught in between jump shots and free throws. My dad was my closest friend.

When I was eleven years old, I was shaken awake in the middle of the night. My mom said "Hurry and get dressed. We're dropping you off at your friend's house. Dad just got called to go to the hospital for a kidney transplant."

Even after that, health problems continued. When I was thirteen, a savage case of gangrene attacked his foot, leaving a deep hole where the skin had been eaten away. With each passing week, the hole kept getting bigger and bigger. His doctor couldn't seem to stop the destruction caused by his diabetes.

When he got home from work, he needed crutches to get into the house. Our time playing basketball together stopped. All he could do was listen to the ball bouncing from inside the house. My dad was discouraged, depressed, and in constant pain. The complications of diabetes threatened a possible foot amputation. Maybe a leg amputation. Maybe amputation of both legs, after sores began developing on his other foot.

His health deteriorated so quickly that, within a few months, he was unable to work anymore. My dad, who had been fiercely independent his entire life, was now forced to depend on others for everything. The loss of independence was crushing for him. I saw his suffering. I heard him crying in pain in his room across the hallway when he thought everyone was asleep. As the days passed, a parasite of darkness and sheer helplessness was ravaging through my body. I couldn't bear to see what he was going through.

A stinging wind was blowing one day in January when the weight of his health crisis, and crushing depression, became a burden too heavy for him to hold.

I was 14 years old when I got off the bus on that afternoon. I walked home from school alone, listening to the snow crunch underneath my feet. I walked up to my room and turned on some music. I opened my math book to get started on homework. And then I heard my brother screaming outside. I ran downstairs and out the front door.

I went into the garage. I looked past the garbage can and saw my dad slumped over with a rope around his neck. I ran out of the garage, and suddenly everything moved in slow motion. The bitter January cold froze my lungs. It felt as if a massive anchor fell onto my chest, and I couldn't breathe. I screamed, but didn't hear a sound. I started running to my friend's house to get help. I didn't hear the snow crunching beneath my feet. I didn't hear anything.

My world used to be a rainbow of brilliant neon colors. Now, it had turned to a deep, suffocating shadow as black as obsidian.

TWENTY-ONE

Many years have passed since that moment. And yet it still feels like someone knocked the air out of me when I think about that day. I still feel my muscles tense up. The sight of my best friend lifeless in the garage is so crisp and tender in my mind. Those scars still feel so incredibly raw.

When I think about him, I grieve all the experiences I missed out on as a result of him being gone. Losing someone you love feels like losing the warmth of the sun. There is a deep, exquisite yearning for what might have been. I have seen firsthand what can happen when someone feels helpless and alone. It's what makes my Google search all the more concerning.

I have been stuck in the fog of depression for almost one year, but only now do I realize how serious it is. I could put a check mark next to almost all of the diagnostic criteria. Depressed mood nearly every day … check. Energy loss and fatigue … check. Indecisiveness … check. Decreased appetite … check. Feelings of worthlessness … check.

I am also experiencing another blatant red flag for depression: a lack of interest in things that I used to love. I email all my running sponsors and let them know that I am dropping all my company sponsors and scaling back my running so I can focus on writing. This is only partially true. What I don't tell them is that my interest in running has evaporated. I just don't care anymore.

For years, I have loved hosting a birthday run with my best friends. We go to my favorite trail in the world, southern Utah's More Cowbell Trail. I always bring a ten-pound birthday cake from Costco, suitable for feeding 48 people. At the trailhead, we put on party hats, then take turns heaving the cake during the trail run. After three miles, we reach the iconic cowbell hanging from a wooden beam near the trail. Then we cut the cake and stuff our mouths with lard and high fructose corn syrup. I look forward to the event every year.

Except that since depression set in, I have no interest in hosting a birthday run. On the morning of my birthday, when I would have normally scheduled our run, I stay home in bed. That night, I glance at Facebook and see that 367 friends had left comments wishing me a happy birthday. I don't read a single one of the comments. I don't care. I feel utterly empty and utterly emotionless.

Depression isn't simply a matter of checking off the boxes on a list of criteria. It affects everyone differently. There isn't a single definition of how depression looks and feels. There is no cookie cutter description of what depression looks like. And this perpetuates the problem by making people think, "I don't look or feel like that person who is depressed, so I must not be depressed."

My particular brand of depression resembles what Emily Dickinson said: "I felt a funeral in my brain." It isn't something that will just go away by thinking happy thoughts. I used to find joy in a beautiful sunrise, or a warm embrace, or the smell of fresh cut grass. Now, I am detached and indifferent to everything that used to bring joy. It's like happiness has filed for divorce against me, citing irreconcilable differences.

But this goes far beyond feeling unhappy. I don't feel sad. I don't feel anything.

Years ago, Mel and I saw an advertisement for a magician who was going to be doing a show at a casino near our house. Since we didn't have anything better to do that Saturday night, we hopped in the car and made the hour drive south for the show.

Once the show started, we quickly realized that this night might be a little rough. This wasn't the kind of magician you would see on late night television. He was the kind of magician you might see traveling the country doing magic shows at colleges. Maybe even high schools. Loud music, occasional pyrotechnics, and his magician assistant/wife's cleavage-revealing outfit were probably the only things keeping him from doing magic shows at elementary schools. His tuxedo looked like it had seen better days, back in the 1980's.

There was the usual pull-a-rabbit-out-of-a-hat trick. There was the saw-the-lady/wife-in-half trick. We didn't have to wonder too much about what was going on behind the scenes to pull off his flimsy illusions. In magic shows, as in life, appearances aren't always what they seem.

The show took a troubling turn near the end. The magician stood on a platform, and lifted a curtain to stand behind. Then some sparklers flashed, and the curtain dropped. And the magician was standing there with a dark red face after the trap door he was supposed to slide through got stuck. We were able to peek behind the curtain … literally. And what we saw wasn't pretty.

For the past year, I've been performing my own magic show, putting on an act to fool the crowd. But the crowd doesn't see what is really going on behind the curtain. What I look like on the outside usually doesn't match how I am feeling on the inside.

I am a fake. I have become an expert at using a mask to hide the sadness, pain, and darkness inside me. I have become a poster child for a phenomenon called "smiling depression." Often, people use smiling as a defense mechanism. Sometimes people hide their depression because they worry about being judged. Sometimes they cover up depression because they don't want to be a burden on loved ones. Sometimes they struggle with perfectionism and don't want to admit being flawed. But faking positivity can become an incredibly heavy burden to carry.

It's no secret that social media creates a distorted view of reality. A picture posted on Facebook or Instagram rarely tells the whole story. The curated appearance of happiness you see isn't often realistic. Yet even though you know you're seeing a distorted reality, you still allow these appearances to shape how you think and feel.

The concept of smiling depression is alarming. It means that you can't always trust someone's outward expressions. It proves that depression can be easy to hide. You can't know the private battles that people are facing. As a social worker for a couple of decades, I've had enough vulnerable conversations with people to know that appearances aren't always what they seem. Almost everyone is facing a private battle.

Henry David Thoreau said that "the mass of men lead lives of quiet desperation." They are desperate for belonging, connection, and hope. This is the riddle I can't quite figure out. I know that many people I come across every day are using a smile to cover up their depression. But if so many people are doing what I'm doing, why do I feel so alone?

Men are especially unequipped to deal with emotions. We aren't taught how to be vulnerable, how to share, open up, and express how we are feeling. Somewhere along the way, we've learned that vulnerability is a sign of weakness.

It is incredibly lonely and isolating to feel like we need to keep our thoughts, feelings, challenges, and heartbreaks to ourselves. We push down all our emotions because we need to be strong.

I hate feeling like a fraud. My friends, my kids, and even my wife don't know about the dark fog that has permeated every crevice of my life. I'm too ashamed and embarrassed to say anything. So, instead, I paint a smile on my face and go about my day, concealing the black despair that is hiding behind the curtain.

TWENTY-TWO

During summer evenings in southern Utah, mosquitoes are like flying vampires of destruction. They aren't the least bit deterred by bug spray. You can take a pre-run shower of pure DEET, and the mosquitoes will still laugh heartily before sucking your blood. Mel and I had a busy day, so it is late at night before we are able to get out for a run.

We put some candy in my pack for a mid-run snack, take our DEET shower, and hit the road. By the light of the streetlamps, I see an occasional bat flying overhead. We ignore the scent of a skunk somewhere in the distance as we talk about how work went today. Within one mile, our clothes are soaking with sweat. In race pictures shared online, people see the glory of a finish line. What they don't see are all the countless unglamorous moments like this spent training for the race.

My headlamp shines ahead, guiding our path along the white line on the side of the road. Suddenly, up ahead, I see something moving in the middle of the street. We stop in surprise, then cautiously begin walking forward. We come upon a pitiful and heartbreaking sight.

A rabbit is struggling with all his might to flee the oncoming humans, and run into the safety of the sage brush on the side of the road. When we get closer, we see that his back legs have recently been run over by a passing car, and his front legs are trying feverishly and unsuccessfully to grip the road and carry him away. Immediately, there is a pit in my stomach. I feel a shiver that makes the hair on my arms stand up.

At the sight of the rabbit, Mel instantly bursts into tears. We stand there watching this helpless animal unable to move his back legs. My first instinct is to just keep running. I want to try to forget the sight of this suffering rabbit. But as soon as that thought enters my mind, I know this isn't the kind of experience I would be able to just forget. Through her tears, Mel says "Cory, you have to do something."

Standing on this deserted road, I wish I wasn't in this situation, but I know Mel is right. I have to end the rabbit's suffering. I walk to the side of the road and grab a large, heavy rock. Mel turns her back, and I drop the rock on the rabbit. I walk over to Mel who gives me a hug and says through her tears, "Thank you for doing that. I know how hard that was for you."

The kids are sound asleep by the time we get home from the run. I am so tired that I should be able to fall asleep within minutes. Instead,

I lay there tossing and turning. I keep thinking about how, deep inside me, there is a broken, suffering rabbit.

I can't keep living this way. Somehow, I need to ask for help. In order for me to move beyond the broken parts of me, something has to die. The endless self-criticism. The doubt. The fear. The shame. I need to let the secrecy die.

I need to have faith that somewhere in the darkness all around me, there are stars.

Knowing what you need to do, and actually doing it, are two separate matters. I know I need to decrease my soda consumption, but I can't bring myself to actually do it. I know I need to go to bed earlier, but it's difficult to actually do it. I'm at the point where I want to tell Mel about the struggles I am having, but I'm struggling to actually do it.

We try to take a trip alone each year. I have seen a few friends share pictures of Island Lake in Colorado. From the very moment I saw a photo of the lake, I knew that I had to see it with my own two eyes.

The small lake is such a brilliant shade of turquoise that every picture looks like a Photoshopped image with the saturation turned up to 100%. The lake is surrounded by towering mountains, grey cliffs, and lush, deep green grass. Glowing patches of snow surround the lake. If you do a Google image search of Island Lake and don't immediately think to yourself, "I'm calling in sick to work tomorrow and driving to Colorado," you are clearly a cyborg.

I showed Mel pictures of the lake. She confirmed that she isn't a cyborg when she said, "I NEED to go there." So our annual vacation has become a road trip to Colorado. When we make it to the Island Lake trailhead, we stuff our backpacks with water, Swedish Fish, and

Doritos, and then begin our trek. We ascend thousands of feet on rugged, technical trails. The elevation is so high that Mel has difficulty breathing.

After hours of hiking, we reach Ice Lake, the last outpost before Island Lake. Ice Lake is a deep shade of blue, making it look like it has been filled with leftover paint from the Blue Man Group. If Vincent van Gogh painted the most exquisitely beautiful landscape in the world, it would look like this.

After a technical ascent up the trail, I see Island Lake with my own two eyes. It is a powerful moment. There is nobody else at the lake, so I sit on a rock and breathe in the stunning scenery. I realize that no picture could ever do justice to just how amazing this spot on Earth is.

We cover the hours, and miles, and thousands of feet dropping back down to the parking lot, then drive back to our motel. In the motel room, Mel looks over at me as we're unpacking our gear. "What's wrong?" she says.

"What do you mean?"

Mel says, "Is there something wrong? Are you okay?"

I don't know what she noticed that prompted her to ask this question. Even though I know I need to confide in her about the depression I am feeling, I didn't intend to have that conversation while we are on vacation. Maybe it was the extreme exertion of the hike that broke down my defenses. Now, there is suddenly an opening where I can let my feelings out.

For a second, I think about Carol helping me with my blisters at Vol State. Sitting on the side of that road in Tennessee, I was shattered. That was the moment it became clear that I can't do everything on my own. When I let myself be vulnerable and admit that I needed help, a light switch flipped on. My back was against the wall. But when I felt Carol's love and compassion, I was able to keep going. It's almost like I traveled 314 miles to learn this single lesson: when life leaves you feeling broken, it's okay to ask for help.

I want to do that again right now. I need to do that again right now.

I fumble with my words. They tumble out clunky and awkward. "I … I don't know exactly what's going on, but lately I've been a mess." When Mel hears this, she looks confused.

"For the past year, I've been feeling my emotions spiraling downward. I feel really discouraged about my health, and it's been hard for me to adjust since leaving the church," I say. "It's like there is a dark fog all around me, and no matter what I try, I can't seem to get it to go away. I just feel empty."

Mel walks over and lays by me on the bed. She puts her arms around me like she is holding a valuable treasure. She tells me how thankful she is that I opened up, and says that she will do anything she can to help me feel better.

I tell her about all the ups and downs of the past year, and she asks lots of questions. I tell her I'm embarrassed about my feelings. I am ashamed that I can't seem to manage the problem on my own. While we're talking, I immediately regret keeping my feelings locked away for so long. The heavy burden I've been carrying is getting lighter. By giving voice to my struggles, it feels like a filing cabinet has been lifted off my shoulders. I admit the reality that I can't do this on my own. It feels liberating to finally acknowledge that.

We talk about making a plan for how to tackle this beast. The conversation with Mel feels like a shooting star rocketing through an ink black sky. It is the first glimpse of light I have seen after standing in the dark for so long. With that sliver of light, I notice something foreign, something I have not felt for such a long time: hope.

TWENTY-THREE

It's not easy letting someone else walk with you into the shadows.

My son is about to leave for Oregon on a mission for the Mormon church. Even though Mel and I have stepped away from the religion, we support our kids in whatever direction they want to go with their religious beliefs.

Many young men and women in the church volunteer to spend 18-24 months away from home teaching people about the church and providing service. In Mormon culture, it is common for someone to speak in church a week or two before they leave on their mission. Following their talk, friends and family generally come over to the house to visit, have refreshments, and give some encouragement to the missionary. I haven't given this tradition too much thought until Jackson's missionary farewell is almost upon us. Then a sense of fear sets in.

The thought of neighbors, friends, and extended family coming to hang out at our house after church triggers a moderate dose of anxiety. I look around the house and get a true sense of all its imperfections.

There are unpatched nail holes in the walls. The gate to the backyard is broken. There is an oddly colored patch of stucco on the back of the house that was crudely repaired after a windstorm launched our neighbor's shed into orbit, then slammed the shed straight into the back of the house. (There is a reason the name of our city is Hurricane.) There is dust on the blinds. There are chewed up baseboards, courtesy of Little Debbie. There is a hole in the carpet of the front room, another home remodeling project complements of Little Debbie. There is a hole in the couch with the stuffing billowing out (Damnit! It's not funny anymore Little Debbie!).

In the week leading up to the farewell talk and home visit, I do my best to patch holes, dust blinds, and spruce up the yard. But ultimately, I have to surrender, stop trying to fix every little thing, and admit that it's okay if everything isn't perfect. Despite my house's imperfections, it will be okay to let our loved ones come inside.

When the highly anticipated Sunday arrives, I watch people filtering in and out of the house. I am enjoying the company of everyone so much that I completely forget about all the little home repair projects I didn't have time to get to. I don't think anyone else is paying too much attention to the little things either. It isn't until everyone has gone home that I realize that I am like my house. I am flawed. And nobody cares. I am perfect in my imperfections.

I look at other houses and think about how they look so perfect compared to my house. Damned if I don't have those same thoughts about people sometimes. They look like they've got everything together. They have absolutely no chewed baseboards. But every house, and every person, has their blemishes. Theodore Roosevelt said, "Comparison is the thief of joy." I can't think of a single instance when this hasn't been true for me.

I was talking with my friend, Holly, about this one night. She said, "For me, it's a relief when I go inside someone's house and see that it's messy. I have four little kids, and I have such a hard time keeping my house clean. I get down on myself if I go to someone's house and it's sparkling clean. No matter how hard I try, I can't ever get my house to be like that. When I notice that someone's house is a little messy, it takes away the pressure of feeling like my house has to be perfect. I know they're just like me. They're doing the best they can. I feel more connected with someone when they let me see the messiness."

Like allowing friends and neighbors to see the imperfections inside my house, I need to let people see the cracks and flaws in my heart and soul. The battle becomes who to tell, how much to tell, and when to tell. I don't want to scare people away by telling them about my struggles.

When Mel and I planned our attack on depression, one of the things on our To-Do list was to schedule an appointment with my doctor to talk about depression. I am a quivering ball of nerves on the day of the appointment. Mel comes with me to provide moral support, and I try to resist feeling like I'm being a burden. We are led back to an exam room and sit on the chairs underneath a rack of ragged magazines hanging on the wall.

As I wait for the doctor to arrive, the anxiousness is making my hands sweaty. My heart is pounding against my ribs like the drum solo in the song "Wipeout." I feel embarrassed and ashamed of the reason I am sitting here in this office. Voices in my head sound like parrots chirping, "He's going to think less of you. You should have been able to handle this yourself. You are insecure and weak. Polly want a cracker?"

For the past year, I avoided telling anyone about the darkness around me, wondering if I was just being overly dramatic. Maybe I was making a mountain out of a molehill and blowing things out of proportion. I didn't want to come off as a negative complainer. Maybe I just needed to give my mood some more time to work itself out. These self-critical thoughts kept me silent and alone. These same thoughts are spinning in my brain while I anxiously wait in the chair farthest from the exam table.

Then the door opens, and the doctor walks in. When he asks, "How's it going?" I have to stop myself from answering with the robotic, thoughtless sentiment, "Pretty good."

I talk with him about the depression I have been feeling. I tell him I am having a tough time working through chronic health issues, as well as coping with the challenges we have faced since leaving our religion.

He asks lots of questions. Then he grabs a piece of paper and draws a circle with the word "depression" written inside. He draws lots of little circles around the big circle. He labels each little circle with words like: grief, self-esteem, spirituality, thinking errors, relationships, behavior patterns, biology/chemistry, social connections, and physical health. He says that all of these things can contribute to depression, and they all need to be assessed.

He talks about how an antidepressant can target the biological/chemical component of depression. Importantly, for most people, a chemical imbalance isn't the only thing triggering major depression. "Sometimes people will come back after a few months of taking an antidepressant, and say, 'This isn't working for me.' We can try some different medications. But a pill alone isn't usually going to fix the issue if they're unwilling to evaluate and make changes in some of these other areas as well."

I appreciate how he is willing to look at the big picture. He doesn't seem rushed. It seems like he actually cares. I recognize that a visit like this isn't the norm. Doctors are on a rigid schedule. They don't have extra time built in for longer conversations like this. Because of those time constraints, they often simply pull out the prescription pad and write an order for a pill. My doctor is taking the time to explain that treating depression usually isn't as easy as swallowing a pill. An antidepressant is one piece of the puzzle. But behaviors, thought patterns, spirituality, social connections, and relationships can't be neglected.

I understand that antidepressants aren't like magic jelly beans. We talk about how it usually takes weeks for the benefits of an antidepressant to kick in. And there are potential side effects like weight gain, sexual dysfunction, and suicidal ideations. Those are some substantive side effects. It's enough to make you think, "Hmmm. Should I take this medication? Is this really the solution?"

"What's frustrating," I say, "is that things are actually going pretty good in my life. Mel and I have never been closer. I have a great relationship with my kids. I have a job I like, and a group of close friends, and a roof over my head. I've got it pretty good. I don't think

I've really got anything too major to even be depressed about." I have been telling myself this story for the past year, and all it has done is keep me feeling lost.

Depression follows you like a shadow, always spewing these insidious lies. It constantly shouts into a megaphone, "You aren't depressed. You don't have anything to be depressed about. You're just being overly dramatic. You're being too sensitive and self-centered." But the only one who can hear the shouting from the megaphone is you. The danger in believing those lies is that they keep you from getting help. Those deceptions keep you stuck in the dark.

Sitting in the doctor's office, we decide on a plan of action. I will try an antidepressant. I will take a closer look at how my physical health issues have been impacting my mental health. I will be more open and honest with Mel about how I am feeling, and let her know if I am struggling. I will do some soul searching and look at what behaviors and thought patterns are keeping me stuck in the dark. I leave the appointment feeling like this is a turning point. I am finally doing something to take care of myself.

Utah is home to a unique brand of Mormonism, with roots that reach into every city, town, and neighborhood. The majority of the state's citizens are members of the faith, and the church is deeply ingrained in Utah's history, politics, and society. If Mormonism was cocoa, Utah would be a Swiss dark chocolate bar with 98% cocoa, while everywhere outside of Utah has the Mormon intensity and influence of a mild Hershey's milk chocolate bar. With less religious diversity, it is more common to feel a sense of exile when people leave the church. Mormons create extremely connected neighborhoods and communities. Losing that connection feels intensely lonely.

Since leaving the church, we've become friends with oth[er] have left the faith. It's the night of my doctor's appointment, and [I] meet up with this group of friends to hang out. We are talking about how our lives have been different since having a "faith crisis." I mention a part of my conversation with the doctor earlier in the day where he talked about how spiritual unrest can contribute to depression. They all agree.

I trust the people I am with, and I know this is a safe place. Our conversation seems like a perfect opportunity to tell them about the imperfections in my metaphorical house that I am beginning to remodel. I tell them about the struggles I have been facing over the past year, how I've felt like I'm stuck in a storm where the rain won't stop. I also tell them that I met with my doctor earlier in the day and that I'm planning to start taking an antidepressant.

As I'm talking, it feels like an anchor has been released. The light shining through the fog just got a little brighter. My friends overflow with support and encouragement. They don't say, "Why don't you just try a little harder to be happy?" Asking someone with depression, "Why don't you just be happy?" is like asking someone with Alzheimer's disease, "Why don't you just try a little harder to remember things?" My friends commend me for my courage.

And then everyone else starts opening up, being vulnerable and personal about how their mental health has been since leaving the church. They talk about rejection that they have faced from their families, cruel comments from friends and neighbors, and the hardships they have experienced while rebuilding their lives.

There is a fantastic book called "Lincoln's Melancholy: How Depression Challenged a President and Fueled His Greatness." Until

had no idea that depression was a lifelong battle for
didn't know his depression was so severe that he
t even dare carry a knife in his pocket.

rom Lincoln that pierced my heart. It made me
DeLorean time machine from Back to the Future
and go give Lincoln a long hug. After a series of career and relationship challenges, Lincoln said to his friend and law partner, "I am now the most miserable man living. If what I feel were equally distributed to the whole human family, there would not be one cheerful face on the earth. Whether I shall ever be better I can not tell; I awfully forebode I shall not. To remain as I am is impossible; I must die or be better, it appears to me."

I am stunned by the bleak despair Lincoln must have been feeling. It normalizes the emotions I've been experiencing. What I find so profound is that this was a comment that he made to his friend. It wasn't something he wrote in his private journal. He wasn't keeping his depression a secret. He never considered that his depression was something that should cause shame or embarrassment. Lincoln was willing to open up and be vulnerable. He was wise enough to bring his depression into the light.

Sitting here, talking with my friends, I realize that I am not alone. That realization loosens the chains around me. Once again, I regret keeping walls up and not letting people into my messy house earlier. Secrecy fuels shame. Vulnerability invites light.

Twenty-Four

I am surrounded by dozens of other social workers, and the room is as quiet as a winter prairie.

In front of the room, our presenter, Amy, says, "I was sitting in a motel room all alone. I pointed the gun at my heart. I took a deep breath. And then I pulled the trigger." As the words escape her mouth, all the oxygen is sucked out of the room.

We are at a suicide prevention training, listening to the penetrating story of a young woman who survived a suicide attempt. She tells us about the feelings of depression that had invaded every aspect of her life. Amy says she felt like a dark cloud had enveloped her, and no matter what she did, she couldn't find a way to clear the cloud away. I shudder as she speaks. She is describing me.

Miraculously, she was found before she passed away from her self-inflicted injury. Her road to recovery included healing many broken ribs, a long stay in a rehab facility away from her children, needing to use a wheelchair and then a walker. It was a long and painful journey. Now, she is standing in front of us, talking about how to prevent such a drastic act. She has turned this trauma into an opportunity to help others and share her message of hope. Amy's courage gives me goosebumps.

Among all her wisdom, one message stands out to me more than anything else. Amy tells us that as she lay in a hospital bed following the gunshot, she was surrounded by her family. Standing there in the group, her mother confided something shocking. "I know how you feel. I've been taking an antidepressant for 30 years."

"I never knew this about my mom," Amy says. She wonders if this information would have been beneficial to her during the times she was struggling. Her family had always portrayed poise. Her parents always appeared to have everything together. So, when Amy was struggling, she was too scared to reach out to her family for help. For me, this is an incredibly eye-opening realization. It is a concept I can relate to, always hiding my darkness behind a mask of smiles.

When I get home that night, I walk into our home office and close the door. I grab a pad of paper and sit writing for so long that my hand hurts. I am not able to talk with my son who is still in Oregon on a church mission, so I decide to write him a letter. I open up my soul and pour it onto those lined, yellow pages. I tell him about the battles I have been fighting, and where I think they began. I explain the sensation of being smothered by a dark cloud, and how, despite my best efforts, I couldn't get the cloud to leave. I write about my pain and fears. Then I tell him about finally building the courage to talk with Mel about how I have been feeling, and then later talk with my doctor. I tell him how thankful I am to finally feel like the cloud is clearing.

Most importantly, I tell him my regrets about keeping these feelings to myself for so long, and about the incredible relief I felt when I was willing to ask for help. I let him know that I will be there to help him if he ever has any feelings like this himself. I recognized that I have been doing the same thing that our speaker's parents had been doing. I have been holding myself together, hiding my weaknesses, and smiling to conceal a heavy depression. I have been portraying the image of being poised and strong despite feeling weak and fragile on the inside. That kind of insincerity hasn't been serving me or anyone else around me. I have to change those unhealthy patterns.

As I finish the letter, I can't bend the cramping muscles in my right hand. But I feel happy about how I have articulated my feelings in the letter. The next step is to talk with my daughters about this issue. I want them to know too. Since I feel like my letter covers all the important points, I decide I will just read them this same letter before putting it in the mail.

We are all sitting in the car ready to leave for a trip. I ask them if they would mind if I take a few minutes to read them a letter before we leave. When I finish reading the letter, they thank me for being honest and open about my feelings. Mel didn't know about the letter I had written. She smiles and says, "Wow, I'm proud of you."

I hope this step helps increase communication and create an environment of trust and honesty. I desperately want my kids to feel comfortable talking with me and asking for help when needed. As difficult as it was, I hope that my vulnerability will help them know that it is safe for them to be vulnerable as well.

TWENTY-FIVE

I find myself in a strange situation: I am a social worker driving to a social worker's office to begin therapy. I am the one who initiated setting up an appointment with a therapist. But now that it is about to happen, I am doubting my decision. I feel like a kid who wants to go on the Space Mountain rollercoaster at Disneyland. That is, until the seatbelt is latched, and the rollercoaster starts speeding down the track. By the time I decide I want to get off the ride, it is too late.

Before my session, I fill out a questionnaire. My brain is on hyper speed, and I have a hard time devoting my full attention to the form. A few of the questions are:

"Can you identify a crisis or event that brought you to seek counseling?"

"What do you hope to get out of therapy?"

"Would you rather bleach your hair neon yellow for the rest of your life, or only have one eyebrow?" (Or something like that.)

I sit anxiously in the waiting room for my therapist while I think back on my responses to the questionnaire. I wonder, "Is she going to say I'm beyond help? Is she going to fall asleep while I talk about my feelings? Is she going to judge my answers on the form?

When she comes into the waiting room and introduces herself, I notice that my leg is trembling up and down. She shakes my hand and says, "Hi, I'm Staci."

I notice that my hands are sweaty and sticky, like I just barely finished licking some raspberry jelly off my fingers right before she walked into the lobby. Gross.

Staci looks to be around my age, early 40's. She is wearing jeans and looks so casual that she resembles someone heading to the sports bar to watch football. She doesn't appear to be a pretentious know-it-all. She seems normal and down to earth.

Since I'm a social worker, I think I'm allowed to admit that some of us in the counseling profession are, well, how should I say this delicately, "unique." Some of us are eccentric or unusual. Some of us have as much personality as a vacuum cleaner. Sure, every profession has "unique" individuals. But if you're going to be sharing your deepest, darkest fears, shame, and hurt, you don't want to do that with someone who is radiating crazy vibes. I don't sense any crazy vibes during our introduction.

This is the most important thing in a therapeutic relationship where work is going to get done. It isn't the school that the therapist went to. It isn't their credentials, or size of the office, or modality of therapy that matters most. It's the innate sense of trust, respect, and connection. There needs to be a feeling inside that says, "Okay, I'm willing to form an alliance with this person to get some work done."

Staci leads me back to her office. There isn't a window or an overhead light in the office. There is muted light from two lamps, a few decorations on the walls, and a desk.

I see one chair sitting across from one couch. I don't know what I'm supposed to do. I think back on my Psychology 101 class where the professor talked about Sigmund Freud, and his client laying on a couch. I assume that the couch is where I am supposed to sit, and the chair is where she sits. I am 99% certain that I made the right seating choice, but the 1% chance that maybe I chose wrong scares me a little bit.

The very fact that I am sitting on that couch in the first place feels like a monumental act of courage. I have been trying to deny that I have a problem for the past year. Then, when I recognized that depression was a concern, I tried to handle it myself for a long time. That clearly hasn't been working. I have been feeling empty inside for so long that I am desperate for change.

I am at the point Abraham Lincoln described when he said, "To remain as I am is impossible; I must die or be better, it appears to me." I am ready to attack depression from as many fronts as I can, including more opening up to Mel, trying medication management, and meeting with a therapist. I am hopeful that sitting in a lamp-lit office, on a couch across from a therapist, will help me get things unstuck.

When I sit down, I can feel my skin begin to sizzle. Now that I am actually here, I feel tremendously awkward and uncomfortable. I hate that I couldn't handle my depression on my own. I barely resist the urge to say, "I'm sorry, I have made a huge mistake. I need to go. Keep the session fee. It's been nice knowing you."

We aren't too far into our introductions when Staci asks, "How do you feel about being a social worker and coming to therapy?"

I think, "Wow, you don't beat around the bush." She seems to read my shame as easily as if I had written, "I'm a social worker, I should be able to do this myself," with a black Sharpie marker across my forehead. The sizzle in my skin grows hotter.

"Well, to tell you the truth, it's kind of embarrassing. I know plenty of people who go to therapy. I refer people to therapy all the time. I've seen therapy change lives. I never hold an ounce of negative judgement toward anyone who goes to counseling. But for some reason, I'm not willing to grant myself that same grace. It's embarrassing because I know about depression, and I help people work through it all the time. But for some reason, I can't seem to work through it myself."

She smiles and says she understands. "I felt the same way when I started seeing a therapist. Being a social worker is hard. We're always helping other people. We go into some dark places with people day after day, and that's usually a heavy weight to carry. Sometimes it's good just to get an outside perspective when you're working through things."

I could be wrong, but I think she just validated that I'm normal, and that how I'm feeling is okay. The muscles in my shoulders relax a little bit. My skin starts sizzling just a little less.

She asks what led me to set up an appointment. I tell her, "I've had some bumps along the way adjusting to a new life away from the

Mormon church. I never realized how much of my life was built on the church until it was gone. I'm also pretty frustrated with my health. I have a huge fear of needles, which really sucks when you're getting stuck by them so often. Those things have really impacted my mood, and I think I've been stuck in depression for quite a while."

I notice myself avoiding the topic of my dad's suicide. I really don't want to talk about it. That was a long time ago, and there are more immediate issues I want to focus on. I am only able to dance around the elephant in the room for so long before this issue finally comes up.

"Okay, so it sounds like there are two main issues you want to focus on. First, you've noticed that issues with physical health are negatively affecting your mental health. And second, since leaving the Mormon church, you've had a hard time with navigating things like relationships with friends and family, and the grief of feeling like such a big part of what shaped who you are is now out of your life."

"Yeah, I think that's a pretty good summary," I say.

And then she hits me with the sucker punch to the kisser. "Have there been any other major traumas in your life that might be connected to how you're feeling today?" Damnit. I'm busted.

After my dad's death, I took that event and set it in a box. Then I grabbed a roll of duct tape, wrapping it over and over across every seam of the box. Then I walked up to the attic and buried the box deep underneath all the other boxes. The experience was so painful that I never wanted to open that box again. The thing is, ignoring trauma doesn't make its impact go away.

I notice my voice cracking when I start telling Staci about my dad. I try to tell myself that I am over it. But my cracking voice is exposing me as a fraud. Because I never dealt with my father's death and locked it away in a box like nothing ever happened, the wounds still feel fresh and raw. Those memories are ugly and unbearable.

As I sit with Staci talking through the experience, my hands become cold and clammy. It feels like harsh bleach is pumping through my veins. I can feel a thick, black rain cloud behind my eyes. As we talk, the overflowing rain finally cracks the walls that I've built around my tear ducts. Water begins to escape. This part of therapy is gut-wrenching.

Staci helps me see that from the very moment my dad died, my teenage brain interpreted that I needed to be strong. I managed to teach myself that I shouldn't show emotions, because if I show emotions, I will be weak. I decided that I needed to be perfect and please everyone so they won't leave me. Being forced to live through that nightmare, I was left feeling powerless, helpless, and out of control. Those are seriously difficult beliefs to admit.

For so long, I have been wearing a mask of strength. What I see behind the mask is shame, guilt, and a pervasive sense of unworthiness. Those feelings pierce my soul, and I feel them as fresh as I did when I was fourteen years old. I want to close my eyes and put the mask back on. But I know this is the time to start being honest, lean into the pain, and put down the mask.

When my dad died, I constructed my own internal Great Wall of China. It was built around my heart to protect all the secrets, emotions, and fears. Then a wrecking ball, also known as a therapist, showed up in my life, ready to dismantle the wall, brick, by brick, by brick.

Twenty-Six

Within the first few weeks of meeting with Staci, I realize that she can see right through me as easily as looking through plastic wrap on a salad bowl to see the vegetables inside. She catches me when I smile to cover up pain. She coaxes me to explore the dark shadows of the cave that I usually try to avoid. She recognizes unhealthy coping strategies and isn't afraid to be blunt and honest in pointing them out. She doesn't let me tip toe around the uncomfortable things.

Sometimes I leave her office feeling frustrated, stuck, or discouraged. Sometimes I feel relieved, light and whole. Since I started going to counseling, I've treated Staci like a psychological mechanic. When I take my car to the mechanic, I am completely at their mercy. I know nothing about cars. I trust the mechanic, and say, "Do what you need to do, however you need to do it." I have trusted that Staci will guide me and show me where to shine my flashlight in the dark parts of the cave.

I still feel the stigma of going to a therapist, but recently something clicked within me. I remembered that even the most elite athletes have coaches. Usain Bolt has been the best sprinter in the world, and yet even he has a coach. There are still improvements he can make in his training, form, and race strategy.

In that same light, I could go to my local gym and hire a personal trainer to help me get in shape. The trainer can prescribe exercise routines, give exercise tips, and provide encouragement. Why is it okay to hire a personal trainer to get in shape physically, but there is a stigma against hiring a therapist to help get in shape mentally? I like seeing Staci as a coach. A therapist is a personal trainer for the soul.

Like working with a good coach, a good counselor can help you see things you haven't been able to see on your own. That outside perspective is advantageous. I know how I see things, and I'm always convinced that the way I see things is right. But it's helpful to get some nudging to look at things from a different angle, as uncomfortable as that can sometimes be.

We have been talking about what it was like to have a parent commit suicide. It is an uncomfortable topic that I have avoided talking about for, well, let me see, every single day since it happened. I hate going to those dark places. Sometimes I fantasize about what it would be like to have a therapy session where we aren't talking about things that sting like a swarm of bumblebees.

Staci: "Did you watch the Utah Jazz basketball game last night?"

Me: "Unfortunately, I did. I can't believe they were winning the whole game, then surrendered the lead with two minutes left and never came back."

Staci: "Really? You can't believe that happened? That's what the Jazz have done in the playoffs your entire life! It's highly likely that you, your kids, and your grandkids will die before the Jazz ever win an NBA championship."

Me: "Okay, I don't want to talk about it anymore. This is only making me more depressed."

Staci: "I completely understand. Some topics are just too painful to talk about, even in therapy. Hey, I was wondering. What bakery has the best cinnamon roll in town?"

Me: "I was born to give cinnamon roll advice. It's my destiny. Carbs are my love language. If love had a taste, it would taste like cinnamon rolls. When you're in a pinch, the Maverik gas station cinnamon rolls aren't horrible. The problem is that sometimes they are overcooked, and they get too hard. A crunchy cinnamon roll isn't worth the calories. Muddy Bees Bakery has some solid cinnamon rolls. Personally, I think their frosting is a little too heavy on the powdered sugar. They also skew high on the frosting to roll ratio. I mean, you definitely don't want to skimp on frosting. Usually, the more the better. But Muddy Bees tends to overdo it just a tad. Okay, I feel like I'm nitpicking right now. They are a solid option. But the gold standard for cinnamon rolls is at Great Harvest. Their cinnamon rolls are always cooked just right. They are always soft and gooey. And the cream cheese frosting is so good that it should be classified as a mood-altering substance and regulated by the government. If I was really hungry, I would probably trade a child for one of their cinnamon rolls. I can even tell you which child I would trade. I would give away..."

Staci: "Hold on a second! Good God almighty! I didn't need a dissertation on cinnamon rolls. Now it's starting to feel like you're just trying to avoid something. Is that true, Cory? What are you avoiding?"

Me: Breaking down in tears, "You're right. I guess I have."

Staci: "What is it Cory?"

Me: "Well, my dad, he…"

Staci: "Go on, you can say it."

Me: "My dad … he … he used to make really good cinnamon rolls too.

Staci: "Okay, you know what? I don't think this is going to work. I'm here to help you. But if the only thing you are willing to talk about is cinnamon rolls, then don't bother coming to another session."

I know better than to try and bullshit Staci with some cinnamon roll distractions. There usually isn't much small talk before getting down to the nitty gritty. It's a testament to her abilities as a therapist that I feel comfortable opening up to her. She asks, "What was it like to be 14 years old and find your dad after he took his life?"

I decide that maybe it is time to actually see what grief feels like. She tells me that it's okay to lean into my feelings. I want to let myself cry, but I can't. I wonder if the well dried up years and years and years earlier.

"I hated when teachers pulled me aside at school to say they were sorry. I didn't want anyone to pity me or feel sorry for me. I hated feeling like I had a secret to keep. I hated feeling embarrassed that my dad killed himself. I hated feeling like my chest had been carved open with a rusty steak knife, and a piece of my heart cut away."

I tell her that I never really felt anger toward my dad. Even though I hated the outcome, I can understand why he made the choice he did. "I think what I feel most is sadness and regret because of all the experiences I missed out on with my dad. He wasn't there when I graduated from high school. He wasn't at my wedding. He didn't see me finish graduate school, and he wasn't there to hold my kids after they were born. He wasn't there to talk to if I had a problem, or if I needed some help. My sadness is mainly because of the fact that he wasn't there."

I sit on the couch with my eyes closed, opening up my heart. I notice tears dropping down onto my shirt as I revisit those painful memories. I guess there is still some water in the well after all.

Staci has a yellow legal pad from Staples sitting on her lap. Occasionally, she looks down and scribbles something on the page. I imagine that if she showed me the piece of paper, it would look like a dot-to-dot picture as she notices the connections between different thoughts and feelings. She points out relationships between experiences and emotions that I hadn't recognized before.

Staci specializes in a form of therapy called Somatic Experiencing, mixed with some Eye Movement Desensitization and Reprocessing (EMDR). It focuses on trauma's connection to both the mind and body. It is about embracing the pain, and experiencing the feelings that we didn't give ourselves permission or validation to experience during past trauma. This contrasts with what I've been doing my whole life, where I take the easy way out and avoid any difficult or uncomfortable emotions. She helps me notice my physical responses as I go back into those painful memories.

Because my eyes have been closed the whole time I've been talking, I am completely disconnected with my surroundings. I forget where I am. I stop noticing the lavender-scented air freshener plugged into the wall. I forget that Staci is even here. I am experiencing the weight of all the emotions I have avoided for so long.

With my eyes closed and talking about all this pain, I not only see darkness, but I feel darkness. It coats me like a blanket of hot tar. I hear Staci ask where I am feeling the pain. I tell her it is stuck in my heart. "What do you notice about that pain in your heart?" she asks.

A distinct picture comes into my mind. "After my dad died, I put a cage around my heart. I didn't want to get hurt anymore. I didn't want to feel anymore. I wanted to disconnect. I let myself detach from emotions. I kept my heart locked up."

She says, "What happened after you put a cage around your heart."

"I didn't feel anymore. I didn't feel any pain or hurt. But I also didn't feel any peace. The cage kept out love from myself and from everyone else."

Then Staci asks a sensitive question that completely alters the way I see my dad's death and the depression that I have been feeling. "So, what do you need to do Cory?"

I feel the hairs on my arms stand up. Through tears I say, "I need to open the door of the cage. I need to let love come in." I sit in silence for quite a while after those words are said. Warm saltwater trickles out the cracks of my closed eyes. I feel a warm hum of electricity all over my skin. I feel alive.

This feels like such a moving, powerful moment for me. I don't want it to be some kind of artificial, meaningless, therapy-sounding nonsense. I know an experience like this could be transformational for me … if I let it. Unless I really act on it, my realization that I need to "let love come in" will be nothing more than a trite saying from a Hallmark card.

Before leaving, we talk about what it would look like to let love in, and specific ways I can do it. I tell her that I need to be more aware of my emotions and be willing to express them. I need to let myself be vulnerable in my relationships instead of keeping distance from people.

The door of my cage is rusty. It's been closed for so long that it has become hard to open. And even when I pry it open, it sometimes slams shut like an old screen door. But before now, I didn't even know I owned a cage. I can recognize thoughts and feelings that I never knew were stuck inside me. This feels like progress.

TWENTY-SEVEN

Middle schools should have a student assembly on the first day of school. A teacher could take a few minutes to talk about the schedule and making sure to get to class on time. The lunch lady could take some time to explain that a lot of meals on the menu include mystery meat. Kids could be notified that when they see "chicken nuggets" on the menu, "nuggets" are actually breaded Styrofoam packing peanuts. Following the lunch lady, the school principal could get up and begin his speech.

"It's a pleasure to welcome you here to Mount Jordan Middle School. When you leave this school, you will have learned a solid foundation of math and science skills. You will be a more creative writer.

And you will spend the rest of your life feeling like you're not good enough. Welcome to a life of trying to hide all your insecurities. Have a great year!"

I didn't have the slightest clue what an insecurity even was until seventh grade. My understanding of insecurities begins after I walk into the building where self-confidence goes to die: the middle school gym. The terror of going to PE class is palpable. The coach begins dividing us up into teams for basketball. He points to one group of pimple-faced kids and barks "You're shirts." Then he points at the group of pimple-faced kids I am standing with. He barks "You're skins."

I consider raising my hand and asking, with my cracking adolescent voice, "Hi. Um, what did you mean just a second ago when you pointed at me and said I was a skin?" But I'm too scared, so I resist the urge. Then I see the guys in my group taking off their shirts. I am instantly mortified. My pubescent body looks less like a human and more like an albino cat. I look less like a teenager and more like a pasty sack of pizza dough.

On the other side of the gym, the girls begin playing volleyball. I am convinced that if the coach isn't joking, if I really have to be a "skin," no girl in the school will ever even think about dating me. I will almost certainly die heartbroken and alone.

Later in the year, I am used to taking off my shirt in front of everyone in the gym class. And every single time it happens, I am traumatized a little more. But my insecurities were about to be compounded.

My English teacher is a sweet, old lady with fluffy brown hair that looks like a bowl of brown spaghetti sitting on her head. Mrs. McGee walks up to my desk as I am leaving class one day. She says, "The school spelling bee is tomorrow. Each English teacher chooses one student from each class to compete in the spelling bee and I'd like to have you represent this class." She talks softly when she says it. She uses the same voice someone would use if their sentence began "Your mission, should you choose to accept it…"

I like Mrs. McGee and I'm feeling pretty badass that she asked me. "Okay, I'll do it." She says she is going to be one of the judges, so I want to make her proud. The next day, my name is called over the intercom and I am told to go to the library for the spelling bee. The kids sitting around me say, "Good luck!" and I feel like a gladiator representing the class as I leave for battle.

In the library, I stand in a long line of kids. "This is the first round. If you get your word right, stay in line for the second round. If you get your word wrong, you can go back to class," one of the judges says.

A few minutes later, I am given my word to spell: "Awesome." I don't need to use the stalling tactic of asking, "Could you use it in a sentence?" I am glad they are starting the first round with easy words so we can get warmed up." I look over at Mrs. McGee and smile with confidence. I want to wink at her as if to say, "Looks like you made a good choice when you asked me to represent the class," but I don't.

I clear my throat. "A W S O M E." No sweat. Mrs. McGee's left eye twitches like she just took a bite of a lemon. "I'm sorry, that is incorrect. You can go back to class now." I am devastated. All the way back to class, I keep running the word over in my mind. "A W S O M E. A W S O M E." I can't believe I have been eliminated in the very first round. I think the judges must have been incorrect when they said I made a mistake. I can't figure out what I did wrong.

Everyone seems surprised when I walk back into the classroom. Someone says, "Wow, that was quick." He might as well have just stuck a dagger in my back. Another kid says, "What was your word?" I stammer. "It was ... Pterodactyl. That one gets me every time."

Middle school is brutal. I hated that age with a passion. I couldn't wait until I was older, when I would grow out of those insecurities and feel comfortable with myself. Surprisingly, when I reached adulthood, my ego got on the intercom. "Houston, we have a problem. These insecurities aren't going away."

Granted, I am infinitely grateful that I don't have to play shirts and skins basketball surrounded by my peers anymore. But even now, experiences come up that nudge my fragile confidence.

I notice excessive insecurities when I walk into Dairy Queen on my lunch break on a sunny Monday afternoon. I step up to the counter right behind a younger gentleman. This guy is in his 30's with perfect, styled hair. He is wearing a nice shirt and tie, and his shoes are exquisitely polished and shiny. I don't know what cologne he is wearing, but it smells like a mix of ambition and Brad Pitt. He is fit and dashingly handsome. I swear, he must be on his lunch break from a photo shoot for the next Calvin Klein commercial. I am 100% heterosexual. And I'm perfectly willing to admit that this guy is stunningly beautiful. If male objectification is wrong, I don't want to be right.

As he steps to the counter, the lady taking his order has a kind of schoolgirl look, like a cheerleader flirting with the high school quarterback. She must be in her 50's. I'm almost certain I see her reach up to wipe drool from the side of her mouth. She tilts her head to the side with a smile and says, "One ice cream cone?"

The man smiles, and his glistening white teeth give me a mild sunburn. He says, "Yeah, I'll have an ice cream cone." Then he says, "I think I'll have an order of fries too," as if he has just made a courageous decision to suddenly live dangerously.

The cashier seems flabbergasted. "Fries too? We call you the ice cream man because whenever you come in, you just order an ice cream cone."

He chuckles as the cashier and the guy behind him, who is quite possibly me, swoon. He says, "My name is Dave."

The cashier beams like a trainer whose French Bulldog just won a blue ribbon at the Westminster Kennel Club Dog Show. "Dave! I'll remember that. I have a friend named Dave."

I can't believe what I am seeing. Dave's smile gets even bigger and he says, "Well, now you have two friends named Dave."

Damn. I wish I had a microphone I could hand him to drop. I think to myself, "Have I ever, EVER been this smooth in my ENTIRE life?" No, I am absolutely positive I have not.

Dave dreamily swipes his credit card, and then leaves to sit down at a table to wait for his ice cream. And fries.

Then I step up to the counter.

I might as well be invisible. The cashier turns around to smile at the female cook behind the window. They are both squealing schoolgirls. "His name is Dave," the cashier whispers to the cook. "I know! I heard!" says the cook who has abandoned the chicken strips in the fryer to watch the whole transaction with Dave.

They stand there talking with each other about Dave for a solid three minutes. Which is just about the most uncomfortable thing ever, since I'm standing right in front of the counter being invisible.

Once the cashier and the cook float back down to earth, the lady behind the counter finally notices my presence. I don't know what to say. I feel incredibly awkward. I finally muster, "Hi. My name is Cory."

She has this kind of less-than-amused face. "Okay. What would you like?" After I place my order, I go sit down to wait for my food. The cashier and the cook don't turn to each other, squealing like schoolgirls, and say, "His name is Cory!" My insecurities and I enjoy a wonderful lunch of overly cooked chicken strips.

Staci tells me that insecurities often begin as a result of experiences we have when we're younger. Maybe childhood trauma, or times when we felt rejected. She hands me a list of the most common insecurities. I am worthless. I am unlovable. I am ugly. I am a disappointment. I'm not good enough. I don't belong. I can't trust myself. I am weak. I am a failure.

I can definitely recognize some of those thoughts in myself. It's no wonder that people try to hide these insecurities. They feel embarrassed. They want to fit in. They worry about what other people think.

Staci asks, "What beliefs did you start making up about yourself after your dad died?" It is a question I had never asked myself before. I suddenly become uncomfortable, noticing my muscles tightening. "I guess maybe I started to feel unlovable. I felt like I wasn't good enough. Maybe if I was more lovable, he wouldn't have wanted to leave."

I instantly feel embarrassed about what I have said. A part of me knows that his decision to take his life had nothing to do with how much he loved me. He was in physical and emotional agony. But I can't deny that my less evolved 14-year-old brain did have some of those thoughts after he died. As the years passed, those thoughts and beliefs planted their roots deeper and deeper. I see that I've gotten so good at being so hard on myself.

I have this inner critic that usually refuses to shut his damn mouth. He looks like a disappointed old man whose car just got egged. He sounds like Robert De Niro. He mumbles in my ear all day long. "Why did you say that? You sound so stupid. Have you looked at your stomach in the mirror lately? Did it ever cross your mind to lay off on the ice cream a little bit? You're an embarrassment. You can't do anything right."

As she starts shining light on these beliefs, Staci helps me see how so many of them are irrational. When I notice this, the insecurities loosen their hold on me. Staci says, "How would your life be different if you let go of some of these insecurities?"

I take a minute to think about her question. "I think it would feel so liberating to let go of these beliefs. I think I'd feel a lot more peace.

During my race across Tennessee, there were many supplies I kept in my pack that I never ended up using. Those supplies took up space and added weight to the pack I was carrying. I had a large emergency blanket, a reflective vest, an inflatable pillow, Mace, and a book with course directions. I didn't use any of those things, yet I continued to carry them mile after mile. When I realized I wouldn't need them, I should have left those things behind.

I am doing the exact same thing in my life: carrying around a lot of useless junk that I would be better off leaving behind. Fear, doubt, self-consciousness, and anxiety add unnecessary weight to the journey. The vast majority of my fears never even happen. Packing that extra weight just doesn't make sense.

The thing is, I know that it's foolish to pack around heavy things like insecurities, doubt, and fear, but to actually take the action of setting those things down on the side of the road is much harder than it sounds. It seems like I have gotten used to carrying that weight and would rather stick with what I know instead of setting those things down and facing the unknown.

I decide that I want to experience some of that liberation and peace that Staci and I talked about. The day after our session, I come up with a plan to take back my control and work toward feeling more peace.

1) Recognize my inner Robert De Niro when he starts piping up. Remember that most of what De Niro says is overblown, irrational, and untrue. Tell Robert De Niro I never liked The Godfather Part II, and he can go to hell.

2) Don't invest so much effort in worrying about what other people think. Dr. Phil McGraw said, "You wouldn't care so much about what other people think of you if you knew how little they did."

3) Comparing myself to other people contributes to insecurities. I can work on being happy with what I have, and who I am.

4) So many of my insecurities are based on perfectionism. I tell myself that if I'm not perfect, then I'm a failure. Instead of evaluating myself based on outcomes, I can evaluate myself based on effort. Outcomes aren't always a reflection of how much effort I put in.

5) In social situations, I think about a friend I want to try to emulate. My friend Josh is outgoing, happy, and personable. Josh has a genuine interest in learning about other people. Josh is comfortable with who he is and doesn't change like a chameleon based on what he thinks other people want him to be. People are attracted to his confidence. When I'm in social situations, I think, "What would Josh be doing right

now?" When I try to emulate his confidence, I start to actually feel it. Sometimes, I start off with little goals like, "I'm going to talk to three new people at this party tonight."

6) I can't base my worth and self-esteem on outside forces. What other people say, my accomplishments, things that happen at work, how many friends I have, my bank account, and my appearance are things over which I don't have control. External forces are always changing and evolving. My worth needs to be based on internal forces.

My friend Maria once said, "My biggest disappointment in life was getting older and finding out that grownups have insecurities too, they just pretend like they don't." For so long, I have been trying to hide how I feel unlovable and unworthy. With the dark storm clouds around me beginning to clear, I am finally beginning to see my worth. It has become so clear. I need to love myself because I am okay. I am whole. I am enough.

Twenty-Eight

A gigantic box arrived on my porch. On the outside of the box, written with bright, colorful markers, are the words "I HOPE ALL YOUR DREAMS COME TRUE!!" I don't recognize the handwriting. There is no return address.

A few days ago, I was looking on Etsy. With Father's Day coming up soon, I typed in the search bar "Unique Gift Ideas." I wanted to get something good for my stepdad. I scrolled past the inscribed keychains. Past the personalized coffee mug. Past the earrings that are beaded into the shape of toilet paper rolls. Suddenly, my finger stopped scrolling. I sat, looking in disbelief, at the most hilarious, disturbing, undeniably amazing gift ever: a cheerful-looking taxidermy raccoon, standing on a table with his hand in a box of Milk Duds.

This leads to two troubling conclusions: 1) There is a person somewhere on this planet who thought it was a good idea to get a dead raccoon, stuff him, mount him in a standing position, and attach a box of Milk Duds for him to reach inside, and 2) I need this raccoon in my life.

Once I see the price tag of this national treasure, my heart sinks. Mel would slice off my eyelids with a bread knife if I spent that much for a taxidermy raccoon. Owning a taxidermy raccoon will now be nothing more than a fantasy.

I share a picture of the furry fella on Facebook with the comment: "I've been thinking about what to tell the kids I want for Father's Day. Honestly, I was going to tell them that all I want is a nice letter. BUT THEN … I saw this taxidermy raccoon eating Milk Duds on Etsy. I know what they're going to say. 'Dad, we don't have $295.' My response will be, 'Well, that's why GoFundMe was invented.'" I figure that someone else might be looking for an incredible gift, so I share the link and encourage people to go check it out.

Twenty minutes passed and I see a comment saying that the raccoon has been sold and is no longer available. It's too much of a coincidence for the raccoon to sell so soon after my post. I'm envious of whichever friend has decided to make their house the raccoon's final resting place.

Five days later, the doorbell rings. I look out the window to see the UPS truck driving away. Then I open the front door and see the box. It's heavy. Inside, there is either enough anthrax to kill a Great Dane, or there is a taxidermy raccoon. Un. Be. Liev. Able.

Ever so carefully, I cut the tape around the seams of the box. I remove a layer of pink bubble wrap. Then I see a tuft of hair. Some glassy eyes like black jellybeans staring back at me. A wry smile permanently affixed to a pointy face. And a Milk Duds box. I stand there for a minute, my mouth gaping open.

I want to hug the sender of this gift and shower them with gratitude. I want to tell them that my life will be forever changed, because no matter what kind of shit storm I face, I will always be able to look over at that taxidermy raccoon smiling at me, and I will smile right back. But I can't thank the gift giver, because to this day, I still don't know who it is.

I think about that raccoon a few months later during a conversation with my friend Rachel. We're talking about the difficulties we've had since leaving the Mormon church. Then she confesses that some life challenges have kept her stuck in depression for a few years now. She says, "I don't really talk about it, but I feel empty inside. Completely empty. It's like I've forgotten what it feels like to be happy."

In all the interactions I've ever had with her, I've never seen anything to give me the impression that Rachel feels this way. She seems happy when we're out on the trails, and when she's hanging out with her family. Only then does it click. Like me, Rachel has been living with smiling depression. It is yet another reminder for me that things aren't always what they seem.

Rachel is like the taxidermy raccoon. She has a smile permanently pinned onto her face. On the outside, everything looks great. On the inside, Rachel is hollow and lifeless. Underneath the surface, there is only darkness. It's terrifying to think of how many people I come across each day who are smiling to conceal an underlying darkness.

The smiling depression, sometimes called functional depression, allows people to push ahead and get stuff done in spite of the thick despair. But just because they might be able to hide it better, that doesn't make it any less destructive.

I saw a comment on Reddit that describes our situation perfectly: "Shout out to the particular hell that is functional depression. This is me. Don't get me wrong, it's better than don't-leave-my-bed-for-a-week depression. I am grateful I can be an independent person. But there is something uniquely horrible about being able to go to work every day, occasionally clean up after yourself, pay your bills, generally put yourself together enough to look like a human being … but that's it. Nothing else. No social life. No hobbies. Constantly battling your mind. And being absolutely fucking exhausted all the time."

Rachel doesn't realize it yet, but by giving a voice to her pain, she is weakening the suffocating grip that depression has on her.

I was so scared to mention to my friends that I had been struggling with depression. Everyone else seemed to have their lives so put together. They all seemed so happy and confident. And yet, when I began to open up about the highs and lows, so many of my friends could relate to the same struggles.

Depression is cunning and deceptive. It feeds on secrecy and tells you that you are standing on an island in the middle of the ocean all by yourself. It dismantles the connections you have with others.

I am sitting in a work conference where the presenter is talking about how important connection is. He says that because this is such a deep human need, we turn to social media where connections are easier and faster. The irony is that while social media has allowed us to connect easier than ever, we have never felt so alone.

I'm writing feverishly on my note pad. "The problem is that those connections on social media are artificial. We only see a curated snapshot of someone's life. This isn't reality! Then we make comparisons to our own lives. We're left feeling inadequate and insecure. Everyone else looks so perfect, while I'm a mess. The time we invest in staring at a screen is time taken away from meaningful relationships."

It's no wonder that increased time on social media correlates to increased depression. We can never live up to the artificial stories we see. Opportunities for connection are all around, but it's easier to stare at a phone or computer while the hours pass by. There is so much life to experience away from a screen.

I love The Beatles. I love Paul McCartney's music. When I hear that Paul is going to be two short hours away in Las Vegas, I casually mention that fact to my family. My kids love Paul and The Beatles more than I do, and they immediately start chirping like a flock of parakeets, saying that we have to go. I admire their enthusiasm, but in order to buy five Paul McCartney concert tickets, I would need to sell a kidney on the black market. While I love Paul, I don't want to end up in Pakistan sitting in a bathtub full of ice cubes with an incision across my back.

I tell them that if they want to go to the show, they will need to buy their own tickets. Without a second thought, they all say they are in. So, they spend the summer working at their minimum wage jobs and tucking away their dollar bills week after week.

At the end of June, we hop in the car, crank up the McCartney station on Spotify, and leave the scorching furnace of southern Utah for the even hotter scorching furnace of Las Vegas. Every time I'm in Las Vegas during the summer, I marvel that mankind can manufacture car tires that don't liquefy into a boiling puddle of rubber while driving on Vegas roads.

We arrive early and can feel the charge of electricity when we walk into the arena. Fans are buzzing with excitement as they anticipate seeing a living legend. Then Paul comes out and begins singing, and thousands of people are instantaneously hypnotized. While he sings songs like "Love Me Do," "Lady Madonna," and "Let It Be," I witness people being teleported through a time machine. They are reliving moments of their lives that were stitched in between Beatles songs. This is most apparent in the kind woman who is sitting next to me.

She walked into the arena, scooted past my family, then sat down alone next to me. I can't help but glance over at her a few times during the concert, and each time, I see her eyes bubbling with tears.

Near the end of the concert, Paul sings "Let It Be." This sweet old lady next to me clasps her hands, holding them tightly together. Her tears continue. In that moment, I know she isn't holding her own hand. She is holding the hand of someone special to her. Someone who isn't with her anymore. But during this song, they are together. The lyrics, "And when the sky is cloudy there is still a light that shines on me. Shine until tomorrow, let it be," have never been more touching.

After the concert, I have the chance to talk with her as the crowd slowly empties out of the arena. She tells me that she has loved The Beatles for more than 50 years. Their music was an immediate connection to the most important times in her life. Seeing her glow is my favorite thing about the concert.

The way this woman experienced the show was a polar opposite to the way the guy in front of us experienced the show. For at least 80% of the concert, this guy was filming songs, watching the show through the screen on his phone. As I watched the videos being recorded on his shaky, blurry screen, I felt sad that his experience was being filtered through an electronic device. How unfortunate that someone would spend a sizable chunk of cash to watch a concert through a shaky, blurry screen. He was missing out on so much around him and he wasn't even aware of it.

I once saw a United Airlines ad online that said, "If you see something that makes you smile, take a picture because it may not be there forever, but the memory of it will always be in your heart and the picture will never change."

I like that. I believe in that. My memory is like spraying a shirt with invisible ink. If I don't take a picture, oftentimes that memory will vanish. When times are tough, recalling a photo taken during a happy time helps pull me out of my funk. Photos are like a direct lifeline to moments of bliss.

You better believe I took some pictures during the concert. But it was good to contrast the experience of the guy in front of me to the lady sitting next to me at the concert. I want to capture those moments that bring me joy, but I don't want to cross the line and go overboard, missing the precious life around me.

I've been investing less time in front of screens, and more time strengthening relationships with people around me. When we get together with our group of friends, we talk more about our ups and downs. Since I first started meeting with Staci, nine of those friends in our group have taken the leap of faith and begun seeing a therapist themselves. When you're willing to be vulnerable, and you set down the phone to actually talk to someone, you realize that you aren't as alone as you thought.

Twenty-Nine

I am surprised to hear Mel's phone ringing. I can't understand why someone would be calling her so late. She's been sitting at the kitchen table doing some charting on her computer for work while I'm in the bedroom getting ready for bed.

I can hear her side of the conversation. "No, I'm sorry. I don't sell those candles anymore." Mel used to be a distributor for a candle company, and occasionally got calls from people wanting to place an order. But she hasn't done that for years.

I know Mel is busy and has a lot of work to finish before bed. But instead of hurrying to get off the phone and back to her charting, Mel keeps talking.

I am touched by the compassion I can hear in Mel's voice. She engages, asks questions, laughs, and talks about what she does at work as a nurse practitioner. Their conversation lasts nearly 40 minutes. After her call, I ask, "What was that all about?"

She says, "It was an old guy who said he was trying to find some candles because they remind him of his wife who died a few years ago. Then he told me that he now has cancer and won't be around too much longer. He sounded so lonely and just wanted someone to talk to."

Mel's kindness moves me. She saw someone in need and took action. For this brief moment in time, she made an impact in this man's life. She didn't regret a single second of the time she spent. Mel was a road angel.

One day during a session with Staci, she says, "Something that really helps fight back against depression is helping someone else, or creating some connection."

I know she's right. I can point to plenty of times in my life when I did something kind for someone or showed some care and concern. Not only did it help me feel connected to that person, but I also felt good inside knowing that I helped.

One year, my employer gave me a $50 gift card to a local grocery store, and I gave the card to a single mom who I knew was struggling financially. One time, I pulled my car over on the way home from getting a root canal to help a guy who was having a hard time pushing his wheelchair up a long hill. One year, instead of having a Thanksgiving dinner at home, our family decided to go serve Thanksgiving at the local food bank.

Those were all easy acts of service. And seeing other people's situations helped put my problems into perspective. Though they were small gestures, they helped me feel a sense of purpose. Creating those connections made me feel like I was making a difference.

I have also been on the receiving side of countless acts of random kindness. Waiting in line at the gas station a few days ago, the guy in front of me bought my drink. One day, I dropped a big stack of papers as I was walking to my car after work, and a lady walked over and helped me pick them up. During Vol State, a teenager stopped to hand me a bottle of cold water during the hottest part of the day.

In the months after Vol State, I've been thinking a lot about my biggest takeaways from that life-changing experience. While out on the roads of Tennessee, I developed a deeper understanding of the power of road angels. During the race, so many random people showed small acts of kindness. To them, I'm sure their actions seemed minor and inconsequential. But as a person who was struggling, those small acts were like spreading a rainbow across a stormy sky.

Sitting on the couch across from Staci, we talk about how you can steer negativity away from yourself and focus that energy on helping someone else. Depression keeps me feeling like a horse with blinders on, preventing me from seeing anything except the pain in front of me. It keeps me stuck in feeling sorry for myself, and only focusing on my own needs and wants. I stop noticing other people's needs and wants.

I know that serving, and making connections with other people, would move me closer to feeling better. But depression makes every day feel like trying to run a marathon through wet cement. I barely have the energy to get through the day. I don't have a spare kilowatt of energy to invest toward anyone else.

I realize that I've been making connection and kindness way harder than they need to be. I've lost sight of my lesson from Vol State: it's the small acts of kindness that make a difference. What so many people are craving is to simply be seen.

This becomes clear one day when I go see my friend Bill. I need to drop off some papers to him at work. My daughter, Dani, is with me. As I park my car, I remember that she hasn't met Bill before. She's heard me talking about him in the past, so I ask her if she wants to come with me so she can meet him.

Dani comes inside with me, and I introduce them to each other. Bill shakes Dani's hand and says, "It's great to meet you! Tell me, what is the best thing that has happened to you today?"

I find his interaction with her to be so powerful. Bill didn't ask an insincere and unthoughtful, "How are you doing?" Which didn't set her up to answer an insincere and unthoughtful, "Fine." Those formalities are completely absent of interest and concern. By asking a question like, "What is the best thing that has happened to you today?" Bill is showing Dani that he cares. He wants to get to know something about her. And this last point is huge: Dani feels noticed.

This brief interaction inspires me. I realize that asking open-ended questions like this could give people an opportunity to move past the curt formalities. It could show that you see someone as a person, not just an object who takes your money when you buy a drink at the gas station. I decide that I am going to start asking more questions like this in my everyday interactions with people, whether it's the grocery store clerk, the janitor at the gym, or the guy checking me in at the hotel lobby.

Despite my good intentions, a few weeks pass, and I just can't do it. Making a more personal connection feels uncomfortable. It feels out of the box, and vulnerable. I am much more comfortable to just get to the counter at the gas station, make a minimal amount of conversation, make a minimal amount of eye contact, swipe my credit card, and get on with my life. Maybe it is social awkwardness showing its ugly head, but I just can't bring myself to do it.

One night, we're hanging out talking with a group of friends, and I mention Bill's interaction with Dani. I tell my friends that even though I want to start making more personal connections with people, I am finding that challenge incredibly difficult. My friends affirm that they sometimes face the same difficulties with social interaction. They also affirm how much it means when someone shows that they care. As a group, we make a pact to put this into action.

After our group pact, I find it easier to try and make connections during casual interactions. Asking a simple question like, "What has been the best part of your day?" while checking out at the grocery store seems to open the door to connection. It is a beautiful thing to watch. Asking a question like this seems to give the other person permission to move past the formalities of their job and reveal more of who they really are. It is like flipping a switch. It immediately snaps people out of their rote, memorized routine, and allows them to let their guard down. Since that time, I have heard some very moving and heartwarming stories.

Once I start feeling comfortable with the question, "What has been the best part of your day?" I want to expand my horizons. I do some research and come up with a list of questions that can form a bridge of connection, even if it's only for a few seconds at the grocery store. Some of my favorites are:

- If you had to pick a character in a movie who is most like you, who would you choose? Why?

- What was your dream job when you were growing up?

- What are you most afraid of?

- What would your perfect weekend look like?

- What is the best compliment you've ever received?

- Has anyone ever saved your life?

- What was your most embarrassing moment when you were a kid?

- What are you ridiculously good at?

- When was the last time you were stuck in a funk? What did you do to get out of it?

- What was the most excruciating hour of your life?

- What is one mistake you keep repeating?

- What is the best piece of advice you've ever been given?

- When was the last time you amazed yourself?

- What is the most physically painful thing you have ever experienced?

- If you had just 24 hours to live, what would you want to do?

- What is your best way to cope with stress?

- Who brings the most happiness into your life?

- What song will put you in a good mood no matter what?

- What is the craziest thing you want to achieve in your life?

I start asking questions like these to my co-workers, patients, kids, and the cashier at Chick-fil-A after I order my spicy chicken combo meal. They help us get to know each other deeper. Showing sincere interest helps people feel seen. It creates a connection.

In my conversations with people, I see more and more that we aren't as alone as we think. Everyone is facing a demon or a doubt. You might not see it, but everyone is a patient in the emergency room with painful wounds on their soul. Everyone is, in one area or another, getting their ass kicked by life. That's just what life does. Knowing that everyone is facing a private battle magnifies the importance of showing kindness to each person I talk to.

I love how Vol State runners refer to the people who do these small acts of kindness as "road angels." The term "guardian angels" just doesn't fit. Guardian angels are too detached and otherworldly. But a road angel is in your face, right here and right now, where the rubber meets the road.

I'm working on being more of a road angel in my everyday life. I can see that when I help bring happiness to someone else's life, it always rubs off on my own. I find healing and happiness through relationships with others. I feel the same hunger for connection that I felt while spending hours alone on the Vol State course.

The guy standing in front of me at the gas station who bought me a drink, the lady who helped me pick up the papers I dropped, the kid who stopped on the side of the road to give me a cold bottle of water ... do they know how much their kindness meant to me? They couldn't. They don't know how their simple gesture lit up my day like a lighthouse. You don't know the impact that your kindness might have. You can't know the immeasurable value of helping someone feel seen. You just need to know that you are making an impact. And that's enough.

THIRTY

The path of healing is not a straight line. It looks more like a graph of the stock market, with its jagged line of gains and losses. I am consistently surprised at how quickly discouragement or depression can sneak up on me, even after long stretches of standing in the light. It's part of what makes the battle with depression so discontenting. Even when you're feeling good, there is always a spark of anxiousness burning at the back of your mind wondering, "Is the darkness going to creep up behind me like a panther and pounce?"

I was running on the outskirts of Bryce Canyon National Park during a race when I noticed the smell of rain blowing in the wind. It didn't make sense. There were some fluffy, white clouds floating above, making the sky look like the opening scene from The Simpsons. Suddenly, the wind began blowing harder. Twice, I had to grab my hat before the wind blew it away. And within minutes the sun was covered by a thick blanket of black and purple.

Rain fell from the sky like an open fire hydrant. My friend, Clint, and I ran as fast as we could, desperately looking for a place to seek shelter. Within minutes, shelter became even more important when lightning began clapping around us. Only a split second stood in between a roar of thunder and the hot, white flash of lightning that followed. It all happened so quickly.

Even when the ten-day forecast on the weather app shows nothing but sun, dark clouds of discouragement and depression can roll in without notice.

I was reading an interview with Bruce Springsteen and he said he has had the exact same experience with depression sneaking up on him. In 2016, I fulfilled a lifelong dream when I stood high in the nosebleed section of the arena, the area where they provide complimentary bottles of oxygen, with my son. The action was far, far below, and the band looked like dancing ants. But I loved every solitary second of the three-and-a-half hour revival that is a Bruce Springsteen and the E Street Band concert.

In front of us, I saw two guys almost get in a fist fight when one yelled at the other, "Hey, sit down man! We can't see!" This was followed by more yelling. Then I watched one of the guys leave the concert, only to come back with a beer that he handed to the guy he had been yelling at ten minutes earlier. That's what Springsteen's music will do to you. In my mind, he is the epitome of confidence, strength, and self-assurance.

Naively, I couldn't understand when I read that Springsteen has had ongoing bouts with depression. The guy takes medication to help keep his mood in check. "All I do know is as we age, the weight of our unsorted baggage becomes heavier ... much heavier," he said. I thought "Wait. Hold on a second. The Boss has unsorted baggage from when he was a kid too?" It was a side of Springsteen I never knew before. His vulnerability felt humanizing. I respected and admired him even more.

It goes to show how powerful and insidious depression can be! No amount of hard work, no achievements, not even an induction into the Rock and Roll Hall of Fame can make you immune from the grip of depression.

There isn't a one-size-fits-all approach to treating depression. What works for someone else might not work for me. For my particular brand of mind funk, therapy and an antidepressant are helping.

I am getting better at recognizing triggers that can break my mood. Overworking myself, feeling stressed, and a lack of sleep make it way too easy for me to slip into negativity. I am working on being kinder to myself when I fall into a slump, and I try to remember that ups and downs are normal.

I am seeing how important it is to notice the storm clouds early and seek shelter quickly. It's okay to slow down and rest. If I wait for my mood to completely fall into the sewer, it is infinitely harder to pull myself out. Preventing mood funk is much easier than treating it.

I make a list of reminders that I can refer to when I notice that I'm standing in a dark valley instead of the top of a mountain. I want these ideas to guide how I think and feel. The items on my Mental Health First Aid Kit are:

- Make an effort to suck the most joy out of every single moment. Make a back-up plan for those times when you get stuck in a funk. Have a person you can call, or a song you can play, or a movie you can watch, or a trail you can run that is guaranteed to get your soul back on track.

- Don't take things too seriously. Have fun! Laugh as often as humanly possible.

- Don't take the little things for granted. You never know what tomorrow holds, so take advantage of today.

- Have patience with others. Be kinder than is necessary. Believe that people are doing the best they can.

- Be a lighthouse for the people who are passing through their storms.

- Make eye contact. Help people know that they are seen. Life is so chaotic that many people feel invisible. Help them feel seen.

- Find people with deep lines of crow's feet around their eyes. These are the people doing the most smiling and the most laughing. The deeper the lines around their eyes, the better. Then work hard to develop some deep crow's feet of your own.

- Take pictures. And not just photos of the good times. Capture the good, the bad, and the ugly. Those snapshots are worth gold. Looking back on happy times will make you smile. Looking back on hard times will remind you that you are resilient, and that things will get better.

- Speaking of pictures, Warsan Shire said, "Document the moments you feel most in love with yourself – what you're wearing, who you're around, what you're doing. Recreate and repeat."

- Energy spent worrying about what others think is wasted energy. You'd be better off investing that energy into making chocolate chip cookies instead.

- Take the path less traveled. Different is good. Embrace your uniqueness. The world needs more people who are willing to color outside the lines.

- It's so easy to get roped into things you don't really care about, and those things can suck up your time like a vacuum sucking up dust bunnies. Time is an incredibly valuable commodity. Avoid becoming overcommitted and stressed by learning to say the word "no." Derek Sivers says, "If you're not feeling, 'Hell yeah! That would be awesome!' about something, say no."

- You are never too old to crank up the music and have an impromptu dance party in the kitchen.

- Be spontaneous. Like H. Jackson Brown would say, "When you look back on your life, you'll regret the things you didn't do more than the ones you did."

- Exercise almost never feels good when you're doing it. Exercise almost always feels good when you're done. Your brain will come up with 4,871 excuses for why you're too tired, or too short on time, or too sore to exercise. Patiently tell your brain to shut the hell up. Then put your running shoes on.

- Be optimistic. Things will work out. They always do. If you look back at all the things that worried you or stressed you out, you'll see that most of the time your fears were unwarranted, and you spent way more time worrying than needed.

- A smile is like a glowing fire in a cold, dark world. Spread that fire as much as you can.

- You are, have always been, and will always be, enough.

THIRTY-ONE

We are taking the kids bowling again. We decide to try a new bowling alley, which turns out to be a colossal mistake. They don't even have a juke box. I'll have to use the $10 bill in my pocket for something else instead of 17 repeats of the song "Africa." My coordination is better than the last time we went bowling, and I don't drop a ball on my toe this time. As I sit on the hard, plastic chair waiting for my turn, I think about how extraordinary it feels to enjoy life's little pleasures again.

I felt like I had been standing alone in the dark for so long. The moon and stars were asleep, simply too tired to shine. A cold wind twisted around me and through me. I was convinced that I was stuck, frozen in a night that was never going to end.

Depression can feel that way. It is impossible to fully understand unless you've had that experience alone in the dark yourself.

It is the winter solstice, the day each year when the night is longest, and the cold is coldest. December 21st sees the least amount of sun, and the night feels like it will last forever. But there is meaning and magic in the solstice. From this moment on, each day becomes longer. The sun rises just a little sooner each morning. The increased sunlight is so gradual that it's almost imperceptible. Even on December 21st, the time when it feels like the night will never end, the sun will eventually rise. And on each of the following days, there will be a little less darkness.

During my lowest, darkest points, it wouldn't have been a consolation to hear that the sun will rise again. Stuck in a never-ending midnight, I might have kicked someone in the groin if they said, "Hang in there, it will get better." That encouragement sounds so blatantly hollow. There's no way I would have believed that musty gibberish. I would think, "Yeah, easy for you to say."

Saying trite, feel good bullshit like this to someone who is depressed could make them turn bright red and breathe fire. Even if it's true, they often don't see the faintest glimmer of light at the end of the tunnel.

When I couldn't stand being surrounded by the black blanket anymore, I told Mel about the struggles I was facing. I started taking an antidepressant that helped clear out some of the murkiness that had been fogging up my brain. I worked on accepting my health and took steps to take care of myself. I rebuilt the foundation of my life that had previously been supported by religion. And I sat across from a therapist who helped me face my demons and heal from the trauma of a parent committing suicide.

Standing in the darkness of depression, I felt helpless and hopeless. I felt overwhelmed with how much work it would take to simply survive until sunrise. Situations over the past two years triggered my downward spiral, but many people have been stuck in the darkness for much, much longer. It is heartbreaking to know that many people can't remember the last time they felt happy.

I am sitting in Staci's office on a Thursday afternoon when she pulls out her notes from our first visit. I feel intense sorrow as she reminds me of where I started. I sit in a warm glow of empathy thinking about how much pain and grief I allowed myself to sit in for so long.

I tell her, "I can't believe it took me so long to realize that showing emotions is a sign of strength, not a sign of weakness. I wish I had told someone how I was feeling, instead of ignoring my feelings and keeping them stuck inside. I really wish I had asked for help."

"You're not alone," she says. "So many people do the exact same thing."

"If I had just dealt with my feelings earlier, I might not be sitting here right now."

Staci commends me for having the courage to walk into the darkness. "You could have kept avoiding the trauma, like you've done your whole life, but you probably would have just kept feeling stuck."

I realize that I survived my winter solstice. More accurately, I survived this year's winter solstice. Depression might always be like a Great Dane, following in my shadow and trying to sneak into my bed to wait for me when I'm not home. Depression might always be sitting somewhere in my car, but I'm going to do my very best to not let him drive.

I have worked hard, faced my pain, learned so much about myself, and now I finally see the sun beginning to rise after a cold, never-ending night. I've been used to seeing the "highs" as good, and the "lows" as bad. In reality, you need the dark to appreciate the light. You need time in the valleys to appreciate the peaks.

It's late, and I tell the kids I'm going to bed. I give each of them a hug and say, "I love you." They give me their typical hug, the way teenagers hug their parents. It feels like I'm trying to wrap my arms around a dead jellyfish. I don't care about the limp hug they return to me. I want them to know and feel my love.

In the bathroom, I'm brushing my teeth. I happen to look at the mirror and notice the most peculiar thing. Above my foamy, winter fresh mouth, I see my eyes. I stop brushing for a second and just look at them. When I look at my eyes, I see me. There isn't a hollow emptiness. I see a spark.

I have a hard time getting to sleep. I lay in bed thinking about how this is the first time in such a long time that I feel whole. I finally feel like I am enough. I can feel my eyes get wet. Hot tears drip down to the pillow. Many nights, I have laid in the dark with tears filling my eyes because I felt lost and helpless. But tonight, the tears flow because of happiness, gratitude, and peace. Through my battle with depression, I have realized a profound truth: I am stronger than the dark.

I think back to the peace I felt on that warm Tennessee night looking up at the night sky. In that moment, I wasn't focused on how dark the rest of the sky was. I was drawn, like the moths that circled the halogen bulbs illuminating the Toyota parking lot, to the light. It almost felt as if the stars were looking down on me, bathing me in their radiant beams. The stars were awake and alive. In that moment, I felt connected to them in a way I never had before. I was one of them.

Now that the darkness around me has cleared, I feel awake and alive. I am made of stars.

THIRTY-TWO

A flat expanse of salt stretches across Badwater Basin and glows like a glistening, white frying pan. At 282 feet below sea level, the basin in Death Valley boasts the lowest point in North America. One July day, I started running on that very frying pan during a race called Badwater. I followed the white line on the side of the road across Death Valley until the road ended 135 miles later. At the end of the road stood a few banners, a few clapping spectators, and a finish line.

In the 1980's, there was a well-known anti-drug television commercial. A guy who sounds like an irritable PE teacher holds up an egg and says, "This is your brain." He cracks the egg into a scalding frying pan, and then says, "And this is your brain on drugs. Any questions?"

At the Badwater finish line, the race director handed me my finisher award, a shiny belt buckle. Standing there accepting my buckle, I felt exactly like "your brain on drugs."

What makes depression so brutal, so overwhelming, so hostile, is that there isn't a finish line. I could endure a sweltering run across Death Valley because I knew that in 135 miles, I would find a finish line. Depression is cruel. It robs you of that certainty.

Depression is an ultramarathon through Death Valley, uncertain if or when the race will end. Depression doesn't give you an award. When you reach the other side of the darkness, there is no celebration, no congratulations, nobody standing there to hand you an award.

Even when you pass through the darkness and make it back to the light, you stand with uncertainty. You know the dark clouds might return. It can feel like a temporary triumph. But it's a triumph, nonetheless.

I'm sitting at Olive Garden with my friend Justin who also happens to be a social worker. We both order the unlimited soup, salad, and breadsticks for lunch. The first bowls of soup vanish quickly. The basket, which once housed six warm, golden brown breadsticks is also vacant. Since the restaurant is crowded, we've been waiting awhile for the waitress. This gives us plenty of time to talk about some of the challenges we're facing at work.

I've been thinking a lot about one of my patients who is in a rough spot. She recently got divorced after finding out that her husband was having an affair. She is financially destitute, having trouble paying for her medications, let alone groceries. Her kids live in different states and don't talk to her very often. There isn't a lot going right for her. It's no wonder she is feeling depressed.

I say to my friend, "How do you help someone who keeps getting hit with blow after blow of stuff like this? She feels like there isn't even a light at the end of the tunnel."

I like what he says so much that I pull out my phone to make a note so I don't forget. "I try to spin situations like that as an opportunity for people to start completely over and reinvent themselves. I like to help them write out their wants and goals. Then we work on breaking each of them down to smaller, more manageable tasks. Otherwise, it can feel overwhelming. You find the little victories and celebrate them. Sometimes it's something as small as getting out of bed or taking a shower. Those little victories are really important when you're working your way out of the pain."

What he says makes sense. When I'm in the middle of a race, I don't do math. During almost every 100-miler I've run, I tend to reach a point around mile 40 when I think "My feet shouldn't be hurting this bad. My legs shouldn't be feeling this sore when I still have 60 miles to go. I think I might be in trouble."

I'm usually around mile 65 when my body says, in no uncertain terms, that it's time to go home. Running is for idiots. It's usually dark, I'm exhausted, and my legs don't want to take one more step. That's when my brain becomes a short-circuited calculator. "DEAR. GOD. I still have 35 more miles to go! I'm only able to walk 20-minute miles. That means it's going to take almost TWELVE MORE HOURS of arduous walking to get to the finish line. I don't know if I can do it."

When I notice my brain going into calculator mode, I try to immediately stop myself. Going 35 more miles when I'm absolutely exhausted is overwhelming. What I really need to be doing is breaking the race down. I only need to focus on the mile I'm running (okay, walking), and finish that mile the best I can. Every mile is a minor victory.

A few bowls of minestrone and a few baskets of breadsticks later, I head back to work. That new note on my phone will come in handy. Next time I meet with my patient, we'll have a new plan of attack. When the dark night of depression feels too heavy and overwhelming, break the race down. For now, only focus on running the mile you're in. The sun will rise. I know because I've seen it.

THIRTY-THREE

As I'm folding laundry in the bedroom, I catch pieces of my daughter Kylee's conversation with Mel. She sounds like she's describing her recent prison escape. Apparently, she could barely breathe and was literally on the brink of dying of thirst. She was sweating so hard that it looked like she didn't even put deodorant on. She sounds so worked up that I leave the laundry and go into the kitchen to see what caused Kylee so much trauma.

The answer: everyone had to run a mile in PE.

I remember so vividly when I felt the same way. I couldn't comprehend how a sane adult with a whistle in their mouth, and a clipboard in their hand, could possibly torture young, impressionable children by making them run an entire mile. There is a special place in hell for PE teachers. Their spot is right next to the people who drive 10 miles per hour under the speed limit in the fast lane, people who talk during movies, people who check out in the 20 items or under express lane at the grocery store with at least 40 items, and politicians.

It's been many, many years since then. Now, I sign up for races, and pay hard-earned money to do something that I once considered punishment. A shift happened when I started thinking about running as a challenge to overcome, instead of a torture to endure. The mere fact that I enjoy running proves to me that the way you think has a dramatic impact on the way you feel. It's easy to look at obstacles and challenges as excuses, but don't take the easy way out. Instead, look at obstacles as opportunities to prove your badassery. It's all about reframing.

In 2018, Mel and I were traveling north on the interstate. I looked over and saw her legs pressed together. "Please, hurry," she said. "If we don't get there soon, I'm going to pee my pants. We were in such a rush to get to the FedEx office before they closed that we didn't even have time to stop and go to the bathroom.

We had decided to make a spontaneous trip to Salt Lake City to see the touring company of the Broadway play, Hamilton. We bought tickets the day before, and our tickets were sitting in a building four hours away from home. We both told our bladders, "Sorry friend, but you're going to have to wait." And then we sped down the freeway.

I felt a wave of panic as we pulled into the FedEx parking lot. Even though we made it ten minutes before closing time, there were no other cars in sight. I darted to the door and was relieved that it was still open. I walked to the counter and provided my tracking number so the package with the tickets could be retrieved.

I could not believe what happened next. As the young man behind the counter started typing in the tracking number, I realized that he had no hands. His arms extended to the length of where elbows would be. He got a confused look and kept typing on the computer. He told me that he wasn't showing the tracking number in his system.

Then he asked if he could see the email on my phone with the tracking information. I handed him my phone and he started scrolling through the email. Then he gave my phone back and started looking through a stack of papers on his desk. He looked in a few envelopes and boxes. And, just so I'm clear on this point, he was doing this without hands!

I couldn't help but say something. At the risk of sounding awkward, I said, "I want to tell you how amazing you are. I honestly can't believe how effortlessly you are doing all these things." My words tumbled out clunky and broken. I was left speechless.

By this time, the office was closed. There was a huge mess with mixed up tracking numbers, and I resigned myself to the fact that the package must be lost. There was no way we'd be going to see Hamilton in an hour. I apologized for all the time I was taking up. He said, "It's no problem. We'll figure it out. I'm not the kind of person who gives up." His kindness, dedication, abilities, and his statement, "I'm not the kind of person who gives up," was deeply moving.

He went back to the storage room again to look around. Five minutes later, he walked into the lobby holding my envelope. It was a beautiful moment of triumph. For situations like this, FedEx should be equipped with streamers that shoot across the office while Journey's song "Don't Stop Believin" blasts on overhead speakers.

But by this time, I was less interested in Hamilton, and more interested in this amazing human. We stood in the lobby and talked about the hardships he has overcome. He told me his name was Julian Pratt. He said he was born without hands and has learned to adapt. He had the kind of smile that literally made his face glow. We took a picture together, and I thanked him for being such a powerful inspiration to me.

We've kept in touch since then. The last time we talked, he told me, "When I was younger, sometimes I used to get mad about not having hands. I got made fun of and felt sorry for myself. Things started changing for me when I decided to look at it like a challenge, kind of like a chance to show people what I'm made of." He feels like living a life without hands has increased his empathy, kindness, and work ethic.

Radical reframing shifted the way he felt. He made a blatant, conscious choice to reconstruct his perspective, and that made all the difference.

Later, as I'm preparing a workshop on workplace burnout, I come across another valuable reframing strategy called "negative imagination" from neuroscientist and author Sam Harris. In an interview on YouTube, he said, "You think of all the bad things that haven't happened to you. So, if you're stuck in traffic, driving to the job you don't like, and you're frustrated, you can think of all the things that could happen to you that haven't. And if any one of them happened to you, you would consider your prayers answered if you could just be returned to this moment."

When I hear this last sentence, I can feel a firework explode in my brain. This is profound. I could be diagnosed with cancer. I could get in a car accident. I could lose someone important to me. If any of those things happened, I would give anything to return to this very right here, right now.

Before I incorporate his reframing strategy into my workshop, I spend some time practicing it myself. I love this way to deliberately redesign thinking and stay connected to gratitude. I notice how negative imagination suddenly minimizes any discouragement or stress I might be feeling. Each time I do it, I am consistently amazed at how quickly this shift can clear away the darkness, even though nothing is fundamentally different about the situation.

There is a yellow sticky note with worn, frayed edges sitting in my nightstand. A long time ago, I was reading a book when I came across a quote by Mary Oliver: "Someone I loved once gave me a box full of darkness. It took me years to understand that this too was a gift."

I didn't quite know what she was trying to say. I sensed that her writing was significant but, to be honest, I didn't really grasp what she was getting at. I grabbed a sticky note to write down her quote so I could think more about it, then set it in my nightstand.

Thanks to some time in therapy, I can now see that my dad's death was a box of darkness. I didn't want the box he gave me. Although there was darkness inside, there were also gifts. Grief, trauma, and depression carry lessons with them.

Inside that box, I received the gift of knowing that I am strong. I am brave. His death, and the depression that eventually caught up to me, taught me about regret. Life is short. I can't wait to say or do something. If something needs to be done or said, I need to do it now. Take nothing for granted.

I learned about the power of forgiveness. The hurt and pain caused lasting scars, but I can find peace in forgiveness.

...portance of creating memories. They are the only ... When I'm caught in the darkness of night, happy ...lowing, bright stars.

...t in the end, only one thing really matters: love. It's ...l love. You have to say it. And you have to show it.

Rumi ...: "Sorrow prepares you for joy. It violently sweeps everything out of your house, so that new joy can find space to enter. It shakes the yellow leaves from the bough of your heart, so that fresh, green leaves can grow in their place. It pulls up the rotten roots, so that new roots hidden beneath have room to grow. Whatever sorrow shakes from your heart, far better things will take their place."

I am sitting in my office filling out some forms, when a woman walks up to my door. She has gauze taped to her arm. Earlier, there were needles in these spots during her dialysis treatment. Now that the treatment is done, she is getting ready to go home. "Hey, could I talk to you for a few minutes?" she asks.

I tell her to come in. She closes the door behind her, then walks up to my desk and grabs the box of tissues. She has only had a few dialysis treatments so far, but during the times I've seen her, she seems to be adjusting fairly well to this "new normal."

Once she sits down across from me, her walls of strength crumble. Both eyes fill with tears. She asks, "How do people do this for the rest of their lives?" She tells me that since starting dialysis, she always feels unbearably tired. She hates that she will have to be coming here every other day for the rest of her life. No time off for good behavior. No breaks for the holidays. No dialysis-free vacations. Nothing will ever be the same.

She pauses after the question. When she asks how people do this for the rest of their lives, I can tell that she isn't trying to imply that she isn't sure she can do this for the rest of her life. She legitimately wants to know how people cope with such a dramatic collapse of the life they used to know.

It's the kind of question for which there isn't an easy answer. There's no quick fix. This isn't a "Take two of these and call me in the morning," kind of dilemma. I take a deep breath and tell her what I've noticed among my patients who seem to thrive despite such a dramatic upheaval of what they used to know.

"I think what it boils down to is trying to find meaning in suffering. You need to find a purpose for the things you're going through." I tell her about a truly transformative concept called "post-traumatic growth."

Essentially, the idea of post-traumatic growth establishes the possibility that we can actively search for and find the good hidden within something horrible. Trauma can bring people together. Catastrophe can lead to growth. Confidence can be found through crisis.

This isn't to say that you'll automatically grow from trauma. It isn't to say that you should seek out disaster. Unfortunately, life has a way of handing out your share of crisis and suffering, whether you're seeking it or not. The possibility of post-traumatic growth implies that strength and meaning can be found amidst crisis, but the growth has to be intentional.

I tell her that this is a conversation that often comes up with my patients. When someone is trying to find meaning through suffering, they usually find out that it's the little acts of kindness, interest, and empathy toward others that really fill their lives with purpose.

There is a consistent theme I hear in my conversations with people who have come face to face with their most daunting challenges. Life is defined by the suffering we endure and the adversities we conquer.

Thirty-Four

Outside the front door, the orange glow of sunrise looks like someone lit the clouds on fire. Past the driveway, there is a car. Past the car, there is a ribbon of road that leads into the unknown.

With the upcoming holiday weekend giving me an extra day off work, I say to Mel "I'm thinking about going on a road trip this weekend. I don't think we've got anything going on. Would that be okay?"

Once a year, I like to escape for a solo road trip. It has become a cherished time to unwind and clear my head. Mel simply can't understand my love for an occasional solo road trip. "That sounds so boring! But if it sounds fun to you, go for it." It does sound fun. It sounds really, really fun.

Mel asks, "Where are you going to go?"

"I'm thinking about just getting in my car and driving and seeing where I end up. I want to take my camera and stop wherever I want along the way to take pictures," I say.

A few days later, I walk out the front door, into the glowing sunrise, get in my car, and give myself permission to get lost.

My car steers me north, past rolling farm fields, and through towns so small that I'm sure everyone knows everyone. There is no need to rush because there is nowhere to go. I find it liberating to not have a predetermined destination, and it feels good to wander.

After many hours, many cracked pepper sunflower seeds, and many bottles of Dr. Pepper, I pull out my phone to look at a map of where I am. If I keep heading northeast, I could make it to Laramie, Wyoming.

Shortly after I got married, I got a letter in the mail saying I had been accepted into the social work program at the University of Wyoming in Laramie. I knew nothing about Laramie when that letter arrived. When I told my boss that I was quitting to go to graduate school in Laramie, he smiled. "Boy, you have no idea how cold and windy it gets up there. I don't think you've got enough lead in your pencil to survive a winter in Wyoming."

Undaunted, Mel and I packed a tiny U-Haul with our meager belongings and embarked on that ribbon of road leading to the unknown. It turns out that I actually did have enough lead in my pencil to survive not just one winter in Wyoming, but two. In our two years there, Mel and I came to love the state and its people. And, as we left everything we ever knew to start a new life together, Mel and I came to love each other even more.

A solo road trip seems like the perfect opportunity to keep following the road to Laramie. I notice long-forgotten memories from that lonely stretch of freeway suddenly flooding my mind.

I remember our U-Haul getting a flat tire at Point of Rocks, Wyoming. Point of Rocks is as grand and majestic as it sounds. This little blip on the map consists of a freeway exit, a rundown service station and, yes, a point of rocks. Point of Rocks is surrounded on the north, east, south, and west by absolutely nothing as far as the eye can see. We watched the tumbleweeds fly by for two hours before someone arrived to fix the flat tire.

I remember passing the town of Wamsutter and talking about how weird it would be if you grew up there, and having to tell people "I'm from a place called Wamsutter." Out the window, we saw antelope standing on the side of the road, completely oblivious to the cars speeding by.

Almost twenty years later, I turn off the radio and think about how much has changed since I last drove this road. By the time I see the glow of Laramie on the horizon, the sky is a velvet splash of purple, only minutes from turning black. The lights of the city on the horizon pierce the darkness like a beacon of stars. Then I feel the hair on my arms stand up. That beacon of stars in the darkness looked exactly the same nearly twenty years earlier from the windshield of a U-Haul.

Almost twenty years ago, I was terrified to uproot our lives and begin a new journey with Mel. I thought to myself, "I just need to get through two years of school. Then I'll be happy. We'll move back to

Utah. Buy a house. Get a job. Start a family. Buy stuff. Then, I'll be happy."

Society handed me a roadmap and said, "Here, follow this map and it will lead you to happiness." But when I followed that map, I found out that it actually led me straight to the city dump. I had a pre-scripted line of stepping stones that I needed to cross like a bridge, with happiness waiting on the other side. I've been done with school for a long time. I have a house, a job, and an amazing family. Yet I still managed to slip into unhappiness and depression.

Looking back on those years in Laramie, we barely had two quarters to rub together. We survived on a steady diet of peanut butter and jelly sandwiches and generic macaroni and cheese. We slept on an air mattress because we couldn't afford a bed. We played Frisbee together because we couldn't afford to rent a movie. Even though times were hard, I look back on those years in Laramie, and I can see that we were truly happy.

It takes a solo road trip two decades after leaving Wyoming to realize that there isn't a designated line of stepping stones that must be crossed to find happiness. The amount of money in the bank account, the level of education, the possessions in the house don't determine happiness.

For the past few years, happiness has felt elusive, like a dragonfly soaring just beyond my reach. Now, I can see that the dragonfly has been sitting on the tip of my finger the whole time. I don't need to wait for something to happen to be happy. Happiness is right here. Happiness is right now.

THIRTY-FIVE

With each step we take, there is a miniature bungee jump happening at the back of the leg, courtesy of the Achilles tendon. This tough cord of fibrous tissue connects the calf muscles to the heel bone. The tendon is responsible for raising and lowering the forefoot and giving the foot its flex. Step in a hole, twist your foot wrong while you're hauling ass down some technical single track, or land wrong after a mid-run jumping picture, and that built in bungee cord could snap. A ruptured Achilles will leave you in the fetal position, sucking your thumb, and sobbing uncontrollably.

There are ways to prevent problems with the Achilles. Stretches and exercises can strengthen the Achilles, and the muscles that connect to it. The more the Achilles is pushed and challenged, the stronger it gets. And then when your jumping picture ends with an awkward, embarrassing landing, those bungee cords will hold strong.

There is abundant scientific literature touting the benefit of exercise for mental health. When we exercise, new synapses and nerve connections are created. Neurotransmitters like serotonin, dopamine, and norepinephrine are released. These chemicals have a positive effect on mood, sleep, and pain inhibition. Endorphins that are linked to happiness and security begin flowing. Running changes our biology and physiology. Not only does the sport alter how we look on the outside, but it alters how we feel on the inside.

Okay, so people who wear white lab coats and have the word "Doctor" in front of their name understand the biological benefits of running on mental health. But the most valuable jewel that running has to offer lies outside the reach of scientists with their EKG machines, their microscopes, and their blood tests. The most valuable gift of running can't be fully understood until you grab a pair of shoes and introduce them to a road or trail.

The most profound benefit of running is this: it introduces us to the pain cave.

Running allows us to willingly push ourselves into uncomfortable situations. You do the things that challenge and strain you. And then, like toughening up your Achilles tendon for the demands of the trail, those challenges make you stronger.

When you run, you dive into the black unknown. You push against the edge of your limits. Our society wants to make things easier. They want comfort. They want to avoid suffering. But not runners.

We embrace the pain cave.

After you hit the wall during a race, after your glycogen is depleted, after fatigue and soreness have overtaken you, and you still have many more miles to go ... that's when you enter the pain cave. As Dean Karnazes says, "There is magic in misery. Just ask any runner."

As runners, we take on challenges knowing that the journey will eventually lead us into the pain cave. We welcome the task. When the going gets tough, the tough remember that toenails are for sissies. We learn what it feels like to suffer and endure. We realize that we are capable of getting through hard times. We become intimate friends with the darkness.

Here is why all of this matters. When life hurls you into the pain cave, WHICH IT WILL, you will have the self-confidence and courage to make it through the night. You'll have the tenacity to fight, to keep moving forward. Running makes us more prepared, not just for physical pain, but also the mental, spiritual, and emotional pain we will undeniably face. We will be stronger for the battles that happen away from the trails.

This benefit can't be overstated. When you run, you willingly choose suffering. You can practice the art of being uncomfortable. It's only when you step out of your comfort zone and into the uncomfort zone that you begin to see what you are capable of. Running allows you to develop a deep conviction that you can endure challenges. Then, when life hands you a heaping dose of unchosen suffering, you have already sharpened your weapons of war against the darkness.

It doesn't take 314 miles to reach the entrance of the pain cave. After nearly a decade of ultramarathon running, that's where I found my cave. But everyone's pain cave is located in a different place. You find it by starting where you are and nudging yourself into the uncomfort zone. Whether you are at the point where a five-minute run seems daunting, or whether it's a marathon or 100 miler, you begin where you are, and then start pushing. Regardless of fitness level, running has a way of teaching us how to suffer. When we face hard times in everyday life, the knowledge that we can persevere is priceless.

Depression is heavy, suffocating, and utterly exhausting. When it takes every ounce of energy just to make it through the day, when simply getting out of bed is an undertaking, the thought of putting on some shoes and running for ten minutes feels insurmountable. Motivation might be nonexistent. What then?

You get behind yourself and push.

You do it anyway. You force yourself to do it, just this one time. You need a spark of action. Then, when you notice yourself making progress, it can turn that spark into a flame. You don't need to wait for motivation. Get behind yourself and push. The motivation might not kick in until later.

One of the most important things I've found to do when you notice depression trying to pull you down below the surface of the water is to fight back with fierce intensity. That requires an intentional choice. You have the advantage. You know depression's game. You know how he fights and know how hard you need to fight back. Fighting depression with fierce intensity is the running equivalent of putting Band-Aids on your nipples: it absolutely must be done.

The tricky thing is that when depression is at its worst, you feel like you don't have the energy to fight back. A lot of times, you don't even have the desire to fight back. As hard as it is, you have to make a conscious choice to do it anyway. Otherwise, depression will slowly and meticulously draw the life out of you.

Have faith that the darkness will begin to fade if you aggressively fight back. A quote from Christopher Woods gives a perfect description of the fierce intensity required when battling depression. "When it's time to fight, you fight like you're the third monkey on the ramp to Noah's Ark ... and brother, it's startin' to rain." Here's my proposition: be the third monkey.

Making it through the night, I can see it now. Therapy and an antidepressant helped clear away the fog of depression. But running saved my life.

Thanks to some debilitating blisters during Vol State, I realized what it feels like to ask for help. Coming across an injured rabbit during a run, I recognized that part of me needed to die. And after spending step after step, mile after mile, year after year in the pain cave, I learned how to suffer. Because of all that practice, I managed to keep going when life barraged me with unintentional suffering. Running literally saved my life.

Runners embrace the pain cave. We are overcomers. This is what we do. This is who we are.

THIRTY-SIX

The salt water dripping down my head and into my eyes stings like acidic drops of lemon juice. An aid station volunteer smiles at me from under his dry canopy and says, "On the bright side, it's only going to get better, because it can't get any worse."

I'm in Virginia running the Yeti 100-mile race. It's the first time I've run a race since Vol State more than a year ago. A mammoth storm front moved in and parked itself right over the race course, and has dumped thick curtains of rain for ten straight hours.

Mercifully, the aid station worker is right. By the time Mel joins me in the evening to pace, the rain has cleared. While we alternate running and walking, Mel provides some distraction from the soreness by talking about the remodeling project we're in the middle of at home. During the week before the race, we worked on lots of yard work, removing old tubs, and demolishing tile around the shower so new tile can be installed. I welcome the distraction as we talk about what still needs to be done at home.

I say, "I'll be honest, I'm pretty proud of myself for everything I've been able to do with you so far. Remember a year ago when you painted the bathrooms and refinished the floors, and I couldn't help you at all because I was so exhausted? That's when my funk was the worst. I could make it through work, but once I got home, I had nothing left to give."

"Yeah, I remember that," she says. "I was kind of mad back then. You didn't tell me what was going on, so I thought you just didn't want to help. I think I would have been totally understanding if you had just said how you were feeling."

I know she's right. I tell her that I have no doubt she would have been completely supportive. I regret that I held back what I was going through.

Then she says, "I feel terrible that you were going through so much with depression and I didn't notice. How is that even possible?"

"Back then, I was the poster child for smiling depression. I was excellent at looking okay on the outside, even though I was a complete mess on the inside," I say. "I was functional enough to barely get through the things that absolutely had to be done, but after that, all bets were off."

The last light of day filters through the canopy of trees above us. We both turn on our headlamps. Mel asks, "What did it feel like when your depression was the worst?"

I'm quiet for a minute, trying to think of a way to explain what that choking darkness felt like. Then I think of a perfect way to describe depression's wrath.

When I was in Boy Scouts, we worked on the Swimming merit badge. Our leader talked about the best way to help someone who is drowning. He said, "You shouldn't just jump in the water to save someone who is drowning. They will be panicking and gasping for air. When you get to them, you'll get pulled under. They will be so desperate to breathe that they will inadvertently pull you down. You'll have to fight and do absolutely everything you can just to stay above the surface."

I tell Mel that at my worst, I felt like depression was like a drowning victim, trying with all his might to pull me into the water and suffocate me. It took every ounce of strength and energy just to keep my head above the surface. It was exhausting and terrifying, wondering if depression would ever let go of me, or if I was on the brink of being pulled into the darkness below.

"Do you ever feel like that now?" she asks.

"Yeah, sometimes I still feel like depression is trying to grab me and push me under the water. Usually I'm able to notice it early and work on it before it gets too heavy," I say.

I've started thinking about depression like a smoke alarm, an alert that something in my life needs to be addressed. Something needs to be verbalized. Something needs to be mourned. Something needs to be said. Something needs to be freed. Something needs to be healed.

For me, depression is often a signal that I've lost sight of the blessings all around me, and I'm stuck in self-criticism. Often, it's an alert that I'm not taking care of myself physically, or that I'm disconnected from my sense of self-worth. Usually, it's a warning sign that I need more connection with others, and that I'm bottling up my emotions instead of expressing them.

When I hear the smoke alarm of depression, it's important for me to quickly take action. When I start to notice dark clouds around me, I can stop the self-criticism. I can eat better and get more sleep. I can talk about how I'm feeling and reach out for help if I need it. Darkness is the teacher.

Wow, it feels so good to drop the fake disguise and talk to Mel about how I'm feeling. She says she has noticed a difference. She smiles and says, "You still have some room to improve and be more open, but I've seen you making a much bigger effort to be more vulnerable."

Mel finishes pacing at mile 64. It's late, and she will go back to the hotel to sleep for a few hours. I thank her for spending the whole day crewing and pacing. She comes over to give me a hug and kiss before leaving. I warn her not to get too close. My clothes smell like someone microwaved a trout in the break room at work, and my teeth have a slimy film of bananas and a ham sandwich from the last aid station.

She gives me a hug and kiss anyway. "It's okay, I smell like a microwaved trout too."

Clearly, my body lied to me. Three weeks before the Yeti 100, I said to Mel, "I think I'm going to back out of the race. I don't feel like my body is ready to run 100 miles again."

She said, "I'm fine with whatever you want to do, but you've wanted to run this race for quite a while. You finally got selected in the lottery, so I think you might regret it if you don't do it."

I figured she was probably right. If I did stay home, I would have wondered, "Are you sure you couldn't have done it?"

Now, I'm in the middle of the race, and it's the middle of the night. Somehow, I've caught an elusive second wind. The way I'm feeling is as rare as a complete solar eclipse. Everything is clicking just right. My legs tick forward like the second hand of a clock, and each step on the trail is as smooth and consistent as a metronome. The miles are passing … dare I say … effortlessly. It becomes clearer with each passing mile that I am capable of more than I realize.

Running an ultramarathon is like solving a Rubik's cube. Sure, plenty of people know how to do it. But to solve the puzzle, you need to memorize a few 12-step algorithms, and do every move just right. Missing one step in the algorithm could mean not solving the Rubik's cube. It might never happen again, but out here on the Yeti trails, I feel like that nerdy middle school kid with buck teeth and a pocket protector who can solve a Rubik's cube with his eyes closed.

When I'm within striking distance of the finish line, I push harder. My stomach tries to warn me to back off a little, but I don't listen. I keep pushing. My stomach says, "Sorry amigo, not smart."

My stomach spasms and contracts, trying to extract everything inside. But I haven't eaten or drank anything for a while, so there is nothing to throw up. I feel vengeful toward my stomach for the stunt it just pulled by trying to vomit. I think, "Ha, ha, the joke is on you."

I resume pushing my pace, feeling the magnetic pull of the finish line drawing me closer. Again, my stomach lurches and says, "I wouldn't do that if I were you."

I keep pushing anyway, but eventually surrender to wrenching on the side of the trail again. And yet, there is something magical about dry heaving by the light of a headlamp at mile 93 while Bruce Springsteen blasts in your ear buds.

The sun is just beginning to creep over the horizon when I make it to the finish line. I felt apprehensive going into the race but end up finishing with my second fastest time ever. Mel hugs me. "Way to go!" she says. "I'm proud of you."

I say "I'm proud of me too."

I am broken.

The trauma of my father taking his life still has an impact on me. I can see how this challenge made me stronger, braver, and more compassionate. I appreciate those attributes, but there is a small hole in my heart that will never be filled.

Two years since leaving the Mormon church, I still find myself cycling through grief, anger, and pain sometimes. As time has passed, I notice those feelings less frequently. I'm farther down the path of my faith journey, and I feel more peace and acceptance. I'm working on integrating my experiences into the person I am becoming. My time in the church formed the person I am, and for that, I am thankful. Some of my closest family members, and some of my best friends are Mormon. Some of the most honest, loving, inspiring, spiritual, and giving people I know are Mormons. My love and respect for members of the church remains, even if our beliefs are no longer the same.

And I still have these health issues that force me to stick needles into my legs or stomach every week. I've been facing my fears and challenging myself. For a while, each infusion was so terrifying that Mel had to do the whole procedure for me. Now, I can do the infusions myself, including inserting the three needles. Even though the needles still make me nervous, I am so damn proud of myself. Each infusion is a victory, and when I'm done, I feel like Muhammad Ali after delivering a knockout punch.

I get discouraged. I get frustrated. The good times are really good, and the bad times can be really bad. I still hear depression ringing my doorbell sometimes. He is standing on my porch looking distinctly similar to Edward Scissorhands, with a suitcase in hand asking if he can move into the spare bedroom. I constantly have to remind depression that I don't have a spare bedroom. He's going to have to go find somewhere else to live.

I've been grateful. I've been resentful. I've been calm. I've been angry. I've been loving. I've been cruel. I've been outgoing. I've been withdrawn. I've been confident. I've been afraid. I've been love. I've been hate. I've been light. And more times than I'd prefer, I've been dark.

I have cracks. I have flaws that run deep. I have imperfections. I am broken. And maybe, just maybe, that's okay.

In Japan, there is a form of art called "kintsugi." When a piece of pottery is broken, the fragments are not thrown into the garbage. Instead, the broken parts are mended together with liquid gold or a lacquer mixed with powdered gold. Imagine a broken bowl or plate fused back together with a brilliant gold glue. Kintsugi takes what was once broken and makes it beautiful. Scars are unique. Scars are valued. Scars are sacred.

When looking at pottery that has been repaired with kintsugi, I am drawn to the spider web of gold streaking across the plate like a lightning strike. That beautiful, unique personality can only be created after it has been broken.

Nobody wants the challenges that life throws at us. And yet it's these very fractures that shape us. Brokenness can be mended. Scars can be healed. I love Ernest Hemingway's belief that "The world breaks everyone and afterward many are strong in the broken places." It is the reason people sign up to run ultramarathons; we know the race will break us. We want it to be hard because the challenge will make us stronger.

We are all broken pieces, and our brokenness fits us together. I think that's why we're so attracted to vulnerability; we bond with someone who is willing to admit that they are broken too. With each other, we can be made whole. It is connection that binds and heals us.

I think life is like a long, long walk across Tennessee. Life breaks us with its blisters, sunburns, and heat rashes that look like you sat down for a naked picnic on top of a hive of fire ants. And yet those challenges are the experiences that shape the race. They are the times when your defenses are shattered, your vulnerabilities are exposed, and you learn the most.

Maybe the reward at the finish line of life is simply knowing that you gave everything you had, you kept moving forward when times got tough, and you loved with every ventricle of your well-used heart.

AFTERWORD

I wrote my obituary in 2020. It was early in the year, when my mind was an electrical storm of terror. I had heard fleeting stories of a novel Coronavirus called COVID-19. I heard about people dying in China. Then I heard that the virus was now in the United States. In Mid-March, President Trump declared a national state of emergency, and the virus was later declared a world-wide pandemic.

Concerts and athletic events were cancelled. Travel was restricted. Hotels were shut down. Stores and restaurants were closed. People were suddenly out of jobs, and unemployment skyrocketed.

Watching the news for a few minutes was enough to initiate a panic attack. The experience of going grocery shopping was unlike anything I had witnessed in my entire life. Many of the grocery store shelves were empty. Shortly after national fear set in, I went to the store and there were no cans of soup. No eggs. No milk. No bread. No packages of pasta. No beans. No rice. And rolls of toilet paper were such a rare commodity that they could have been traded on the New York Stock Exchange.

I could not believe what I was seeing. It was the kind of stuff I had read about in history books. I kept thinking that this couldn't be real. I imagined that at any moment, I was going to wake up and say to Mel, "You will not believe the crazy dream I just had! People were fighting over toilet paper!" But the dream kept going for so long that I eventually determined this must be reality.

The fear consumed me, polluting my thoughts and actions. Working in health care, I was involved in meetings that were terrifying. I was working with COVID-positive patients. I knew people who had died from the virus.

I had been doing my weekly immunoglobulin infusions, but my immune system was still severely compromised. I worried that if I caught the virus, my body might not have adequate defenses to fight it off.

When I watched the news, I felt my chest tightening like a tight rubber band around my lungs. I saw overflowing emergency rooms. I saw stories of people dying in the hospital alone because the hospital was on lockdown and would not allow any family visitors. The images on the news were overflowing with discouragement, fear, and death. I decided to type my own obituary just in case the Grim Reaper was hiding behind my shower curtain waiting to introduce me to his sickle. Luckily, I've been able to avoid the reaper so far.

2020 was a difficult year for a lot of people. For some, it was the overwhelming emptiness of being isolated from friends and family. For some, it was problems with finances, or employment. For others, it was failing health, death, or grief.

I am writing the afterward of this book on December 21, 2020. It is one of my favorite days of the year, the winter solstice. Today, I will make it through the shortest period of daylight, and the longest night of the year.

I take a lot of comfort in knowing that tomorrow the night will be just a little shorter. The day will be just a little brighter. This is how it works when you're experiencing a dark night of the soul, too. It doesn't automatically go from dark to light, like flipping on a light switch. Change occurs incrementally, almost unnoticeably. But whether you notice it or not, the light does continue to grow.

It's a perfect day to finish writing this book. It feels meaningful and symbolic, like recognizing that the past has been dark, but tomorrow will be just a little warmer, just a little brighter.

The process of writing this book was unlike writing my first two books. Initially, I resisted bearing my heart and soul. I wanted to stay away from the things that are personal, the things that are hard to discuss. Eventually, I conceded that this was the story that needed to be told. I can't remember how many nights I stayed awake until sunrise writing, then deleting, then writing, then deleting. I can't remember how many mornings I woke up before the break of dawn doing the same thing. Writing this book was like having a stubborn tapeworm inside me that had to be painfully yanked out, inch by inch.

The value that I've found in telling my story is the connection it has brought with others who understand what it's like to be stuck in the pain cave. You never know what darkness someone may be hiding behind their smile. So many people recognize the dark night that just won't end.

If you happen to be stuck in a cold night right now, I can't tell you that everything is going to be okay. I just want to tell you that you're not alone. You are not alone. Keep moving down the dusty road. Run the mile you are in. Soon, the stars will shine, and you'll find your own pebble of peace. At some point, the light is going to shine again, and someone is going to need to hear your story.

I think back on the mighty Mississippi River that I crossed on the first day of Vol State. I used to think I was kind of like that river, following my own individual course through life. A river is defined by its boundaries, the banks that confine where the river can flow. A river has a name, and a route. It has a beginning, and an end.

Once a river reaches the end of its route and flows into the ocean, it can realize an exquisite truth: it has always been more than a river. It is water.

We are more than our own separate rivers; we are all water. We are all connected, all a part of something bigger than ourselves. We are all kindred spirits, each of us battling our own private wars.

I want you to join me in beginning a conversation about the masks we wear, and the struggles we face. All around us, people are suffering in silence. I want to be part of a movement that makes it okay to admit our weaknesses and ask for help. I want you to step out of the darkness with me and stand with others who are broken like us.

Let's band together to become a tribe of road angels. Let's take a risk and ask for help when we have blisters on our soul that we can't fix on our own. Let's make connections, and help people feel seen. Let's complement the stranger at the grocery store. And let's grow some deep wrinkles around our eyes from laughing too much. Let's stay up way, way too late staring at the stars. Let's embrace the beauty and the pain of this precious gift called life.

In this moment, you might be the one shining the light, or you might be the one searching for it. Wherever you are on the path, keep reaching and keep fighting. Together, we are stronger than the dark.

ACKNOWLEDGEMENTS

This was a difficult book for me to write. It went through many, many rewrites as I tried to get the words to accurately paint a picture of my thoughts and feelings. I owe many people a debt of gratitude, and a pan of warm cinnamon rolls, for their help and support along the way.

To Maria Bradley, and Jaren Jenke: thank you for your insights and suggestions as I polished the final draft. This book is better because of you.

To Luke Thoreson: I swear we are on the same author wavelength. You have an innate ability to understand my ideas and intentions, and your perspectives always help give the stories more depth. I look forward to returning the favor for all the help you have given me over the years.

To the running community, and to our post-Mormon friends: thank you for helping me find belonging during the time I was feeling lost and alone.

To Staci Sandvik: it was terrifying to begin therapy. You helped me feel safe. Thank you for walking with me into the darkness. I would not be where I am without your understanding and guidance.

To Stephanie Cook: you helped give the book direction and focus. I could not have hoped to work with a better editor.

To Laz: I can't count how many times I cursed your name over the course of my 314-mile journey across Tennessee. But your race helped me understand the importance of being a road angel, the value of asking for help, and the power of vulnerability.

To Jeff and Carol Manwaring: you did more than share your underwear with me and help patch my blisters. You showed me love during the time I was fragile and raw. I feel so fortunate to call you friends.

To Jackson, Dani, and Kylee: this is a difficult acknowledgement to write. Words are inadequate to describe how much you mean to me. You help bring meaning and purpose into my life. My love for each of you is like a burning sun of warm, white light.

To Mel: you are the picture of unconditional love. I am so grateful for your help with my health and infusions. You tolerated countless all-nighters and have always shown complete support while I wrote this book. You helped put me back together when I was feeling broken. You have my heart. You are gold.

You know what? Thanks!

With so many books out there to read, I'm thankful you chose this one. Seriously. Thanks! I sincerely hope that the universe rewards you with good karma in the form of skin that never chafes, microwave popcorn that doesn't burn, Jeans that always fit perfectly, and a chocolate fountain to sit next to the toaster in the kitchen.

If you enjoyed Stronger Than the Dark, here are a few things you can do now that you've finished the book:

- Write a post on social media. Facebook, Twitter, and blog posts are awesome ways to let people know you liked the book. 80% of the time people choose a book, it is because of a word-of-mouth recommendation!
- Tell a friend you think would like Stronger Than the Dark.
- Go pick up a copy of my first two books, Nowhere Near First, and Into The Furnace.
- Head over to www.coryreese.com and subscribe to the mailing list for new articles, upcoming events, and epic cinnamon roll recipes.
- Leave a review on Amazon, Goodreads, or wherever you bought the book. Reviews help a ton.

I sincerely appreciate your awesomeness. Consider this a virtual hug. Sincerely, Cory

BONUS:
BOOK CLUB QUESTIONS

- What feelings did this book evoke for you?

- Why do you think exercise is such an effective tool to combat depression?

- What parts of the story could you most relate to?

- Why do you think a stigma persists against depression despite a heavier focus on mental health in society and media?

- Did the book change or enhance your view of depression?

- Why do we sometimes find it so difficult to express how we really feel inside?

- Cory talks about an experience staring up at the stars during Vol State and feeling an all-consuming, pervasive peace. Has there been in a time in your life that you have experienced that feeling?

- As a social worker, how would you imagine Cory addresses depression differently with patients now that he has experienced it himself?

- What experience in the book hit you hardest emotionally?

- What are some specific things you could do in your life to be a road angel?

- Cory talks about how "life is defined by the suffering we endure, and the adversities we conquer." How does this apply to your life experiences?

- Cory talked about his Mental Health First Aid Kit. What would be in your Mental Health First Aid Kit?

- What is a situation in your current life that you may be able to see differently through "radical reframing?"

- How does the idea of "smiling depression" effect the way you interact with others?

- During Vol State, there were many supplies Cory never ended up using, but he still carried them around, taking up space and adding weight to his pack. What things are you packing around in life that you would be better off leaving behind?

- The book talks about kintsugi, repairing broken pottery with liquid gold, and how we can "become strong in the broken places." What challenge have you experienced that ended up making you stronger?

- What are some of your favorite ways to start feeling better when you notice yourself in a funk?

CPSIA information can be obtained
at www.ICGtesting.com
Printed in the USA
LVHW050905160621
690358LV00018B/3699